Dividends and other corporate actions

Gabriel Jablon

Second edition

To my friends and my family.
They truly are the best.

Contents

1

Introduction

What are dividends?

Dividends are the most common way to remunerate shareholders. They regularly make the headlines for being whether too much generous or not generous enough toward shareholders. For the public force that has stakes in public companies, dividends are a way to improve a public budget that is anemic in time of rising public spendings.

Dividends are one of the main sources of shareholders income, the others being share repurchases[1] and profit reinvestment[2].

[1] A share repurchase plan is the action of buying shares of the company on the open market. Share cannot be kept on the balance sheet, they must be cancelled or distributed as payment to employees.

[2] Profit reinvestment means that a company that generates profits will retain them on the balance sheet rather than spending them.

Those three income sources are three examples of corporate actions. The differences between dividends, share repurchases and profit reinvestments are the impact on the stock price. In effect, the impact of dividends on the stock price cannot be determined in advance, while a share repurchase program and a reinvestment of profit will mechanically make the stock price go up[3].

On average, it is estimated that dividends represents half of the shareholders income, on the longer run[4]. For this reason, dividends are often viewed as the sweet retribution for shareholders commitment, and **companies will seek to increase its nominal amount in a progressive manner**.

On the contrary, reducing the amount of a dividend will often be seen as bad news for a company. This move is a cash-conservative measure and thus will be interpreted as a distress signal for the concerned company.

What are dividends: a definition

A dividend is retribution to a company's shareholders. It is proposed by the board and submitted to the shareholders vote at the Annual General Meeting. Most of the time, shareholders follow the board recommendation. This revenue is the redistribution of part of the companies' profits to its shareholders, in whatever form the company decides to choose (cash or stocks).

Some cash or stock payments are called "dividends" but they are not technically dividends in the sense of profit allocation: they are bonus shares for Annual General Meeting attendance, incentives to bring the stocks during a merger, etc. Those payments are often made in stocks.

---

[3] Share repurchase plans decrease the number of stocks. A profit, if positive, will increase the fundamental value of a stock and the market price for this stock will follow.

[4] Dividends reinvested.

Last but not least, it is perfectly correct to use the word "payment" for a dividend that is paid entirely in stocks. As we will see later, every dividend has a payment date, a record date and an ex-dividend date.

Different theories

There are **two basic theories** that explain why companies pay dividends. **First**, every successful company will face the challenge of allocating the excess of cash it produces. In effect, the money a company makes during a year will remain on the balance sheet of the company. Past the normal accumulation of cash, every extra dime on the balance sheet is seen as a cost if that money is not used for a purposeful use (investing). **That idle money bears an opportunity cost that must be handled by the company.**

The other theory is the signaling theory: paying a dividend can be interpreted in two different ways:

- Paying a dividend can be seen as **positive** since it denotes that a company has strong cash generating capabilities and thus good financial health. Bad companies will be identified as such since they will not pay any dividends because they cannot afford it;
- Paying a dividend can also be seen as an acknowledgment, by the company board, of the absence of investment projects and thus for future prospects. In this case, paying a dividend rather casts a **negative** image.

So what theory can we trust? Market reactions following dividend payment have been studied numerous times, so has been the signal theory[5]. However my experience showed me that paying a dividend is never seen as a lack of possible investments or made to lighten the balance sheet. The signal theory has a larger impact on the stock price, and a reduction or suspension of

[3] We suggest you read the article "Signalling with dividends, stock repurchases, and equity issues", by Paul Asquith and David W. Mullins, Jr.

the dividend is seen to have disastrous impacts on a company stock. It is not actually the dividend cut that has an impact on a share price[6] but it often triggers or closely follows a stock rout.

Why companies cut their dividends

Dividend cuts often happen during a period of durable stress. A company that has financial difficulties will try to maintain as long as possible a dividend at par with what it usually pays. Along with the difficulties, they will try to reduce the dividend's impact on the balance sheet by reducing the amount, or paying it in shares (no cash outflow), or both (in 2015, Santander reduced the amount from EUR 0.60 to EUR 0.20 and decided to pay partly the dividend in scrips[7], versus what they had announced earlier (100% in cash)).

Eventually, **a company may have to cut its dividend entirely**, should the difficulties increase. Oftentimes, a dividend cut is predicted by the market at an early stage. In effect, difficulties of a company result in earnings lower than usual, degraded capital ratios, etc. Should earnings continue to deplete due to a weak environment (a company that is exposed to the prices of commodities that faces a drop in the commodities prices) or due to the company's poor performance (for example: large losses), **the stock price should decrease along**.

If the dividend remains steady and the share price decreases, *Ceteris Paribus*, the stock yield[8] will increase in large proportion that will be seen as unsustainable in regards of the company performance. **If the yield is seen as a kind of interest rate**, the farthest it is from risk-free interest rate, the more dangerous it is. So **when yields increase because of a drop in the share price,**

---

[6] We will see later the process of "detachment" of a dividend.

[7] It is an option to elect the dividend in stocks. This major concept will be explained in Chapter 2, "the different nature of dividends", "scrip versus cash".

[8] Yield = dividend amount/stock price

it means that the company is losing in value, and expecting a dividend is increasingly risky.

So dividend cuts being a sign for economic difficulties, and markets being said to adjust quickly, markets often price a dividend along the stock value. If the market price of the dividend is too low considering what the company is used to paying, it means **that investors do not believe that the current level of the dividend is sustainable** and they expect the company to cut their dividend[9].

Timing of dividend reduction: some examples.

Here is an example of how a large company (in that case, a bank) will manage its dividend payment to reduce its cash outflow, in a period of troubled times.

Our example, **Banco Popular Español**, a Spanish bank, faced the three steps of a poorly managed dividend communication: before 2011, it was paying cash dividends. After being unable to pay a dividend of the same amount it previously had paid, it cut it by 30%. It then proposed a scrip alternative in 2012, before cutting it to zero in 2013.

18-Jul-2014	Stock with Cash Alternative	30-Jun-2014	Interim	0.009913
19-Feb-2014	Stock with Cash Alternative	30-Jan-2014	Interim	0.039588
01-Jun-2013 (estimated)	Cash Dividend	--	Final	0.000
26-Jun-2012	Stock with Cash Alternative	15-Jun-2012	Final	0.213634
13-Apr-2012	Stock with Cash Alternative	12-Mar-2012	Interim	0.106817
11-Oct-2011	Cash Dividend	10-Oct-2011	Interim	0.132269
21-Jul-2011	Stock with Cash Alternative	24-Jun-2011	Final	0.132269
09-May-2011	Stock with Cash Alternative	12-Apr-2011	Interim	0.131055
12-Jan-2011	Cash Dividend	11-Jan-2011	Interim	0.129920
11-Oct-2010	Cash Dividend	08-Oct-2010	Interim	0.194880

Illustration of dividend page of Banco Popular[10]

[9] More details on the market value of the dividend are given in chapter 2: "Market value versus intrinsic value of a dividend".
[10] Source: Eikon

Here is another example from a (Spanish) bank: on the 9th of January 2015, Banco Santander announced the conclusion of its EUR 7.5 Bn capital increase and subsequently cut its dividend for the FY2015 by two thirds.

An example in an insurance group: on the 26th of February 2014, RSA Insurance Group announced it would cancel its dividend payment and raised GBP 800m through rights issue.

On the opposite, **pursuing the payment of a dividend despite economic turmoil is not a guarantee that the stock will not be sanctioned**. For example, when Delta Lloyd announced its half year results on the 11th of August 2015, they confirmed that they would pay an interim dividend at par with what they had paid since 2011 and that the dividend was more than largely covered by operating business. However, on that day, the stock tumbled from EUR 16.51 to EUR 13.17 (that was a 20% fall in a single day). It happened because Delta Lloyd had missed market estimates on its solvency ratio[11] and that shed doubts over the capacity of the company to meet future solvency ratio targets.

Illustration[12]:

Delta-Lloyd interim comment about dividends: *(extract from the Half Year results, published on 11th of August 2015)*

> **Dividend payment**
> Based on our dividend policy we decided to pay an interim dividend of € 0.42 per ordinary share, which is unchanged from 2011-2014. The dividend may be paid entirely in cash or entirely in shares, as the shareholder prefers. Shareholders who do not state a preference will be paid the dividend in shares.

[11] The solvency ratio is a regulatory ratio that is an indicator of the riskiness of an insurance company. It is computed by dividing the capital by the written premium. The higher it is, the more the company can cover any potential claim.

[12] Source: Delta-Lloyd interim report.

And the following market reaction:

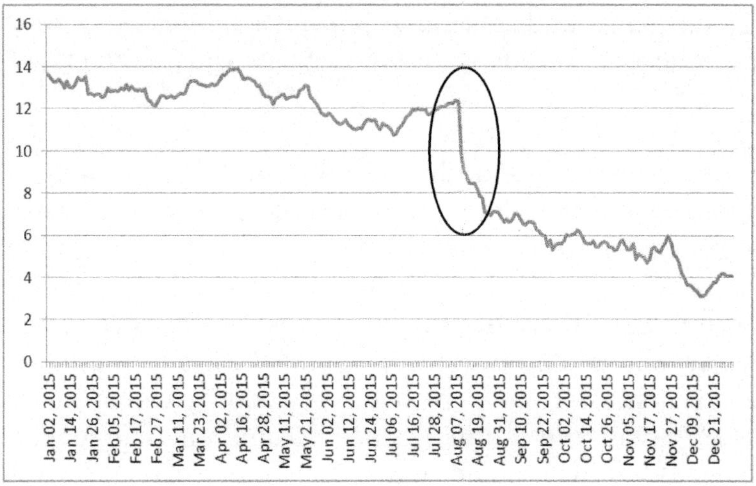

Oops.

What investors will be looking for?

The yield

We already have evoked the yield as an indicator of the sustainability of a dividend. **The yield is the division of the yearly dividend by the market price of the stock**. It can be computed in real time with the value of the stock fluctuating, and the expected dividend for the full year (or the divswap value). Personal investors will seek high yield stocks as an investment tool, since they will consider dividends as revenue.

However we will see later that the payment of a dividend has no impact on shareholders' wealth, it is just a transfer of wealth, since the stock price is adjusted by the amount of dividend that is paid[13]. **The only interest we can see in seeking yield is when**

[13] Modigliani and Miller developed a theory, saying that a dividend is neutral to the shareholder point of view: whether the amount is higher or below the amount the shareholder expected, shareholders will adjust their portfolio

a large shareholder, often the main owner of the company, **receives a significant part of his revenue from the dividends**. He will not sell shares in order not to lose ownership or pay taxes on capital gains, and will only live out of dividend gains. The examples are numerous in the industry: cosmetic giants, global breweries, etc[14].

However, this kind of shareholder behavior is not common since the majority of single shareholders do not draw a significant part of their revenue from dividends.

The other use of dividend yield is to assess the risk of a company, almost like using CDS spreads[15]. If one compares the dividend yield of a stock with the dividend yield of its sector (comparing with the company's peers), one can assume whether the dividend is overvalued, undervalued, or correctly priced. If the dividend yield is too much different from its peers, it can be a sign that the dividend is at risk of being cut, and thus the company is in poor financial health.

Also, the absolute value of the yield can say much about the company. **One can evaluate the global risk of a dividend to be cut compared with the market risk-free rates**. For example, a dividend yielding 12% when interest rates are at zero must draw suspicion. Only high yield sectors can afford that (mining, oil and gas companies,...) but they are at high risks. In any cases, market operators will check for the yield compared to the sector the company belongs, in order to assess the risk.

As a conclusion, we can note two elements:

- **First**, from the agency theory, paying a dividend has absolutely no impact on the shareholder's wealth and thus **must not be seen as an investing tool from our point of view**. However it is a good tool to assess the relative risk attached to a dividend;

---

according to their strategy. See in the introduction "Other corporate actions: share buybacks" and in chapter 2, "market reaction to dividend payments".

[14] L'Oreal, Sabmiller, for examples.

[15] The higher the spread, the higher the risk.

- **Second, individual shareholders are not well informed of the risks of dividends**: they will often seek high yielding stocks, which are also the riskiest.

For information, for 2015, the average yield was around 2% in Europe, the biggest payers were banks (5%), oil and gas companies (8%)[16].

Growth

Many companies promise to deliver a growing dividend to lure investors into buying their stocks. As we have seen above, **the level** (or future level) **of a dividend should have no impact on the investment decision** of a potential shareholder, since the dividend must not be considered as an income. However the promise of a dividend growth has an impact on the way one evaluates dividends, and more generally, on the investment decision.

In effect, many companies will explicitly communicate on their "commitment" to regularly grow their dividend (for example, they will say each yearly dividend grows by 4%). **This kind of statements must be taken with serious care** since oftentimes, those declaration are made without any realism in the promises. At best, those statements are made without any wrong thoughts and based on the assumption that the company will grow and increase its profit forever. **Executives often underestimates the real costs of paying dividends, and during downturn phases, paying a steady dividend can become a heavy burden**. Especially, most companies have the will to increase the dividend payments, but they have a limited horizon of analysis. A 20% dividend increase for a mature company is not realistic.

Generally, hasted declarations are caught-up by economic realities and the corrections are even made by the same person who made the statement in the first place. **Dividend growth must be consistent with economic growth and**

[16] 2015 figures

sectorial/financial regulation applied to the industry. Let us not forget that dividends are paid to the shareholders after every other stakeholder has been paid.

The example of HSBC disclosing their dividend policy[17]

The signaling theory states that a good company will make expenses to signal to the markets its quality, and a bad company will not do that since it cannot afford it. Dividends are one of the example literature gives to illustrate the signaling theory[18], and this is why it can be difficult to estimate dividends: dividends estimations are in fact a mix between financials and discretionary views of the company.

Let us see the change in communication that HSBC Group has faced over the last few years.
On the 2013 annual report of the bank, published on the 24th of February, 2014, commenting the financial year 2013, the CEO stated (emphasis ours): "We continued to demonstrate our ability to generate capital to grow our business and to support our progressive dividend policy, cementing our status as one of the highest dividend payers in the FTSE[19]."

That was a little bit too optimistic, and the wording changed the following year:
On the 2014 annual report of the bank, published on the 23rd of February 2015, commenting the financial year 2014, the CEO stated: "We are also restating our commitment to grow the dividend. To be clear, the progression of dividends should be consistent with the growth of the overall profitability of the Group and is predicated on our ability to meet regulatory capital requirements in a timely manner".

---

[17] Source: HSBC annual report, 2014 and 2015.

[18] It is one example that is, curiously, not *that* common.

[19] FTSE 100 or Footsie : the benchmark index for English stocks.

In this case, the statement underlines that regulatory demands are to be met before any dividend is paid[20].

Other corporate actions: free share attributions

Lastly, **there are ways of retribution that are often called, and considered as, "dividends" while they actually are not**. One example is free shares, whether it is for rewarding attendance at an event (rewarding the attendance of the Annual General Meeting), rewarding the loyalty of a long lasting shareholder (from time to time, a company will offer a percentage of free shares for existing shareholders) or as incentives to shareholders to offer their share during a merger (when the merger closes, the shareholders receives free shares).

For example, during the merger of Lafarge and Holcim (the French and Swiss concrete giants), shareholders have been offered one free share of the newly created company for every 20 share of the newly created company they owned. De facto, the company increased its total number of shares by 5%.

Another example is the rewards Air Liquide performs from time to times to its shareholders. They are offered a 10% bonus share, and that is one reason why Air Liquide **is seen as a good investment** by individual shareholders.

Should it be seen as a good investment?

Increasing the number of shares does not increase the wealth of shareholders: following that kind of distribution, shareholders will have more shares with each having a little less value than before.

For example, let us take a company with the following characteristics (cur. EUR):

---

[20] See chapter 7, "Financial institutions", "Capital reinvestment".

Market capitalization = equity value	800
Profit for the current year, to be distributed	45
Number of shares before a 10% share gift	100

Before the profit attribution and the 10% share gift, each share will be worth 8.0€[21]. If there are 100 shareholders, each shareholder will have an 8.0€ wealth.

After the profit attribution and before the 10% share gift, each share will be worth 8.45 €. Each shareholder will be rich of 8.45€.

After the 10% share gift, each share will be worth 7.68€, but each shareholder will have 1.1 share, making each shareholder be rich of 7.68 x 1.1 = 8.45.

The risk attached to giving away free shares is the problem of dilution: even if giving away free share is costless for the company, the number of stock increases, so **at constant earnings, earnings per share decrease** and the amount of new stocks to be given the following year also increases, and so on. It is an inflationary spiral that can be offset only if the company buys back its own stocks (see below).

Other corporate actions: stock split

This type of corporate action perfectly illustrates why paying a dividend in stocks does not increases the wealth of shareholders. This corporate action simply consists in increasing the number of stocks quoted on the market in order to provide more liquidity. The split ratio can vary from 2 to several hundreds. A split by 2 means a twofold increase in the number of stocks.

[21] 800 euros / 100 shares

Despite what companies may say, a stock split is not a dividend (or at least not considered as a dividend by us).

Example:
In 2006, Royal Bank of Canada (RBC) performed a stock split (1:2) it called "stock dividend" while highlighting the two terms were equivalent.

We put below an extract of the Q&A[22], published prior to the split, aimed at shareholders, to explain the reasons behind a stock split (emphasis ours).

> **Q.** ***What is a stock dividend?***
>
> **A.** A stock dividend is a common way to implement a 2-for-1 stock split. Each RBC shareholder will receive one additional common share for each whole common share owned as of the close of market on the Record Date of March 27, 2006. Since the number of issued common shares after the stock dividend will double, the market price at which the stock trades is expected to be reduced by roughly half, while the value of each shareholder's investment remains unchanged.

Screenshot of RBC explanation of what they call "stock dividend".

Our conviction is that RBC called it a dividend to reassure their shareholders on the impact of this operation on their wealth. But in the end, as stated by RBC, each shareholder's investment will not change post-split.

Other corporate actions: share buybacks

Share buybacks (or share repurchases) is **a program launched by companies which want to limit the loss of value of their stocks**, whether it is due to dilution (the company gives away free stocks, makes a capital increase, etc.) or bad market performance. When it can afford it (meaning its balance sheet carries a lot of cash, possibly thanks to divestments), a company can choose to buy its own shares, instead (or even in parallel) of paying dividends.

---

22 http://www.rbc.com/investorrelations/pdf/stock_div_q&a.pdf

When a company launches a share buyback program, it discloses **an amount and a duration** of the program (example: they target a total of EUR 1.0bn share bought during a period of 3 months), then the shares are bought on the open market. The shares are then cancelled, the price of each share increases (Ceteris Paribus), the number of outstanding share diminishes, and the dividends that are paid after the program represent a smaller total amount.

The use of share buybacks is often marginalized and not considered much more than what it is. However, **while emitting new shares to give them away as gifts must not be considered as dividends, share repurchase program should be**. In effect, while free distribution has no impact on the shareholders wealth (it is just a monetization of the company's performance through a transfer of wealth), **share repurchases benefit everyone**: those participating in the program will be able to sell their shares at a higher price, and every other shareholders that do not participate will see their ownership increase along an increase in the share price (Ceteris Paribus).

Share repurchase programs are also a good way to offset financial difficulties with delaying the cash outflow to the future. **The following strategy, while a little bit technical and not reassuring for the shareholder, it totally legitimate**: 1) in a stressed financial environment, a company will choose to pay dividends in hope that financial markets will not sanction the company for its weak performance. 2) Being unable to afford it, it will pay those dividends in shares. 3) The following year, when the financial performance catches-up, the company buy-backs its own shares (the same number of share it emitted a year earlier).

Share repurchase programs are such a powerful tool that many people are in favor of the end of dividends as they are today and the generalization of share repurchases as a way to remunerate the shareholders.

Last but not least, the impact of share repurchases must be taken into account when computing the cash available for paying dividends, since the share the company repurchase are also, like dividends, paid with cash from its balance sheet.

Are dividends meant to disappear?

If you build the cost/gains matrix of dividends versus share buybacks, you will notice that dividends are always sub-optimal compared to share buybacks. For this reason, we think that dividends should disappear as a mean of shareholders' remuneration, and be replaced by share buybacks.

Benefits:	Dividends		Share buyback programs	
For a shareholder	If cash dividend: - every SH obtain cash (+) - dividend is taxed (-)	+	Participating shareholders: - get cash (that can be tax-free) (+) - are reluted (+)	++
			Non participating shareholders: - are reluted (+) the value per share they own increases (+)	++
	If scrip: Participating shareholders get - shares (+) - whose value is reduced due to dilution (-)	/		
	Non participating shareholders get - cash (+) - taxed (-) - get diluted (-)	-		
For a company	If cash dividends: - destruction of capital without any upside	-	- destruction of capital (-) - offset by reluction (+)	/
	If scrip dividends: - get diluted	-		
For the state	If cash dividends: If the state does not own any share: - taxes (+) And, if the states owns shares: - taxes (0,5+) - cash (0,5+)	++	- No gain if the state does not own shares (/) - the value per share they own increases (+)	/
	If scrip dividends: If the state does not own any share: - nothing (scrips are tax free) (/) And, if the states owns shares: - stocks (+) - gets diluted (-)	/		

Total gain	/	++++

The companies' strategy: constant payout versus constant amount

When deciding to the dividend strategy, companies have several options available:

- **A constant/increasing dividend**: the company will **emphasize on the amount** of the dividend and will seek to smooth the dividend payment over time, whether leaving it unchanged (see for example Delta Lloyd) or increase it over time. The increase can be of a small amount if the company has a more mature profile (for example: industrial, tobacco firms) or has not seen a recent cut or a large amount if the dividend was cut recently.
    - For example, following the 2008 economic downturn, many companies have drastically cut their dividends, and due to stressed economic environment that lasted until 2012, and then followed by recent recovery, dividends have only started to increase recently. In order to catch-up with "normal" levels, some companies have seen dramatic recent increase (sometimes 50% increase or even 100% increase[23]);
- A company can stick to **a fixed payout ratio, or will have a target payout ratio:** every year, the **company's dividend policy will be to pay a fixed percent of its profit**, without (theoretically) take into account the number of shares or the amount of profit. In practice, in case of weak performance, and if it is possible, the company will increase the payout ratio. A notable example is Société Générale[24]: the dividend it pays is highly volatile and closely follows results. It is understandable since the bank has a strong culture of market finance activities, whose earnings are very volatile;

[23] Example: UBS. Full year 2013 dividend: CHF 0.25. Full year 2014 dividend: CHF 0.5.

[24] See the chart and pay close attention to the year 2011.

- Or **pay a dividend along the randomness of its results**. In those cases, a close analysis of the performances is needed, and the sustainability in the longer run is not relevant since the company will automatically adjust its dividend.

NB: companies can do both strategies: communicate on the amount and on the payout ratio. It is however quite risky if it cannot maintain both in the future

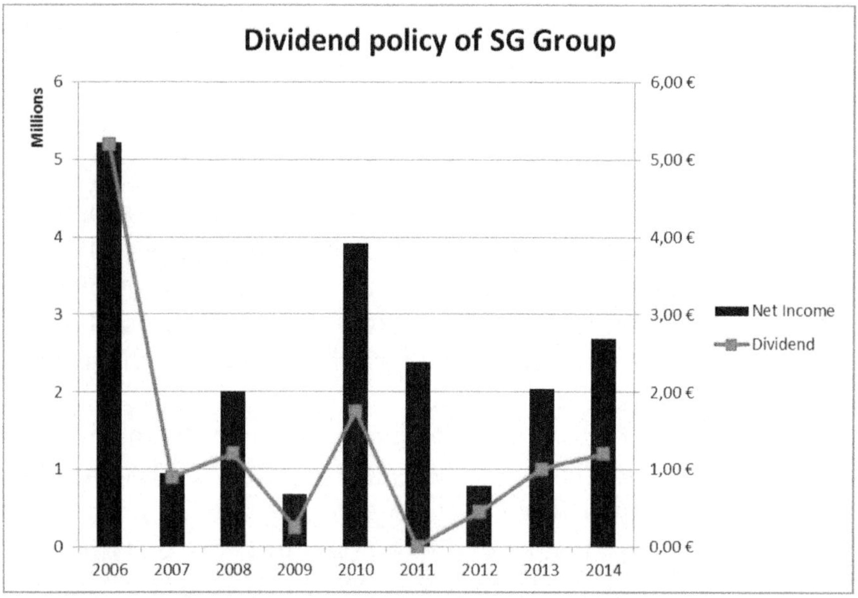

Dividend policy of Société Générale since 2006

Comments on the chart
The chart illustrates a very interesting points that is particularly relevant for dividend estimation:
1) In 2006 and 2007, Société Générale paid 100% of its profits as dividends;
2) From 2008 to 2014, Société Générale changed its policy to

"only" pay 50% of its profit, on average;
3) The exception is 2011 where it paid no dividend (the reason is that the bank was in capital shortfall and needed to save cash[25]).

Other dividend reductions: the "cut"

When evaluating a dividend for a company, one of the main risks is the most feared: **the cut. Evaluating a dividend is not an easy exercise because dividends are financial assets whose value is not continuous**. In the part on the timing of a dividend reduction, we highlighted the numerous steps before a cut. However in many times, those steps are not followed and the company jumps directly from paying a dividend to not paying any dividend at all. A dividend cut happens faster than market players expect. One reason is that many companies (especially British ones) cannot use stock dividends as an alternative to pay dividends (the shareholders will ask for cash since there is no incentive to opt for stocks) and thus will go from a cash dividend directly to no dividend at all.

The other reason is that, generally speaking, when a company undertakes measures to reduce the cash burden of a dividend (reducing it slightly, paying it partly in stocks etc.), it is rarely the first measures: it is 100% sure that others more drastic ones will follow. An important rule is that **when a company cuts its dividend, it is more unlikely than likely that it will increase its dividend during the following quarters/years**. So like for stock valuation, a terrible situation is in many occasions the first step for an even worse situation.

Last but not least, **periods of intense financial stress can lead to uncertainties on the ability of a company to pay a dividend, and generate high volatility on the value of a dividend**. For example, on the 30th of June 2014, when BNP Paribas announced it would plead guilty and be fined 8.9 Bn

[25] See Chapter 7 "Concrete application", part "Financial institutions", first paragraph

euros by the Department of Justice for *illegally processing financial transactions for countries subject to U.S. economic sanctions*, market immediately forecasted that no dividend would be paid and the value of BNP dividend for the full year 2014 dropped to zero. BNP Paribas later declared that they would pay a dividend at par with what had been paid the previous year (EUR 1.50), and in cash. The value of the dividend bounced back immediately.

2

Links between dividends and financial markets

Market reaction to dividend payments

There are two types of impacts on the stock price around a dividend payment. The first one is the impact following a dividend announcement, the other one is the impact when a dividend is effectively paid.

As we have seen earlier, **a dividend announcement has rarely an impact of its own**. It is the results that come along and market expectations, which makes the impact. To be more precise, it is the difference between the expected results and the actual results. **When results are better than expected, stock price increases, when they are lower than expected, stock price decreases.**

Let us now focus on **what happens when a dividend is paid**. When a dividend is paid, it means that shareholders receive it on their brokerage account. It can be in cash, in shares or both. The day the dividend is taken into account (we say it goes "ex-dividend", meaning that the share is traded without the dividend), the stock price will lower of the amount of the dividend. **This mechanism is made to avoid arbitrage opportunity**: if the stock price was not adjusted, everyone would buy stocks just before the dividend detaches and benefit from a risk-free profit. Hence, **by lowering the stock price, we are remembered what dividends really are: a transfer of wealth along a monetization of profit attributable to shareholders.** Before and after the detachment, the total wealth of shareholders is the same.

Dividend indexes

The value of a regular index is the value of the freefloat of each stock it is composed of, weighted by their relative value. The formula is:

$$\text{Value of an index} = K \times \frac{\sum \text{freefloat} \times \text{cap} \times \text{price of each share}}{\text{Divisor}}$$

With
K = level of the index at initiation (example: 1000 points for the CAC 40)
Cap: the capping factor of a share, if any (if a company represent more than a certain % a STOXX sub-index, its freefloat is capped).

The divisor is computed by indexes providers, its formula is not known in advance and depends on the total number of each stocks and their value. That number is recalculated according to corporate action that can occur, for example the increase of the number of stocks of a company, following a capital increase.

A dividend index is an index whose value is computed with the dividend paid by each of the stocks it is composed of. For example, the DivDAX® (property of Deutsche Börse) contains the 15 companies of the DAX that have the highest dividend yields.

Given the freefloat of a company (the number of stocks that are publicly quoted) and the divisor of the index the company is quoted on, **a financial analyst will compute the value of the index in dividend points.** Instead of taking the stock value, the analyst will take the value of the dividend. That value of the dividend changes with several factors over time, so the dividend index value will change.

The total value of the dividend index is thus computed with the same formula as above:

$$\text{Value of a dividend index}$$
$$=$$
$$= K \times \frac{\sum \text{freefloat} \times \text{cap} \times \text{gross nominal value of the dividend}}{\text{divisor}}$$

So the computation is made for each company, and in the end, by summing Dividend Index Points (abbreviated **DIPs**) you get for each company, one gets the total value of the dividends in the indexes. **Each time a dividend is paid, the remaining value is computed with the value before the payment minus the value of the payment.**

The exercise of analyzing each dividend, computing their values in DIPs and summing these values is a work that every equity analyst has to make, **it determines the value of the dividend index and the fundamental value of the index, retreated from the dividends.**

That work is called "bottom-up" since you start with every single stock (the "**bottom**") and then deduce the value of the dividend index (the "**up**").

Last but not least, the special dividends that we mentioned earlier are said to be 100% adjusted in these Bottom-ups. In the dividend index you just built, the value of those special dividends is **zero**. It is very important to take that into account, because large special dividends can represent a huge amount if not adjusted.

Impact of dividends on the indexes

Indexes value is computed with the weighted average value of the stocks that compose them. As dividends are part of the intrinsic value of a stock, each dividend that is paid has an impact on indexes value. There are two main types of indexes, regarding their treatment of dividends:

- **Regular indexes**: when a dividend is paid, the index value decreases by the value of the dividend in the index (the amount of the dividend multiplied by the relative value of the stock);
- **"Total Return" indexes**: the dividend is virtually reinvested in the indexes so there is no impact of dividend being paid. The index's value does not decrease for every dividend that go ex-div. The only example in the European indexes is the DAX.

The other case the dividend is not taken into account when it is paid, is for special dividends. Special dividends are said to be "fully adjusted" in the indexes, so their impacts on regular indexes is zero (note: in some indexes, special dividends are adjusted by their net amount. For example, in the EURO STOXX

50, French special dividends are adjusted by 70%. Technically, the SX5E is diminished by 30% of the amount in DIPs).

At first sight, the reader will not see much difference between a regular dividend and a special dividend. But actually **the difference is impactful since large stocks that pay large dividends can modify by a large amount the value of the index just by paying a special dividend instead of a normal one.**

Example: for the individual shareholder, receiving 1 euro in form of a regular dividend or 50 euro cents in form of a regular dividend plus 50 euro cents in form of a special dividend is the same thing. In both cases, he will receive 1 euro and the stock will lose 1 euro of value. However, for the market maker that valuated the index with the regular dividend at 1 euro, its position will appear to be valued at 50 euro cents if half of it is a special. On large positions, it can lead to tremendous losses.

A focus on special dividends

One must differentiate **regular dividends** paid through the regular process of production of the firm and **special dividends**. As we will see in the next chapter[26], a special dividend is considered as an "**extra**" dividend (whether of stocks or of dividends), and for that reason is not taken into account in the value of the indexes. On the bottom-up you will build[27], you can insert a line when a special dividend is paid must **it must be adjusted at 100%** (and thus it represents zero DIPs). This step is very important in the building of bottom-ups since it states that you have noticed a special dividend is to be paid, but chose to adjust it.

---

[26] Chapter 2, "The different nature of dividends", "Regular dividends, special dividends", and following.

[27] See Chapter 3, "Dividend index valuation: the interest of building bottom ups".

Market value versus intrinsic value of a dividend

Dividend swaps, dividend futures

Before the mid-2000, dividends were not tradable financial assets, there was basically no dividend computation, and the whole performance of equity indexes was made without taking into account the impact of dividends. **Under the impulsion of market makers, futures providers (ex: Eurex) started to market financial derivatives whose underlying assets were dividends.**

The two mainly traded tools on dividends are dividend futures and dividend swaps. It exist dividends futures on single names or on indexes, while dividend swaps are made on single stocks. It is a derivative tool used to play the exposure on a predetermined stock's dividends. However, not all stocks have dividend futures, only the most liquid stocks do (usually the largest capitalization of indexes).

The value of dividend futures and swaps on single stocks can be considered as the "market value" of dividends, since they represent a quotation of the estimated dividend to be paid. It is not a very liquid market since there is not necessarily a quotation. Most of the exchanges are made "**Over The Counter**", so the most recent price is only available when there is a transaction or when a market maker asks for a price on the market.

Fundamental value versus divswap value

Usually, the value of divswaps/dividend futures carries a discount compared to the fundamental value of the dividend (the one computed by fundamental analysis, which we will see later[28]). That discount represents the risk one takes, by owning a dividend. **The lower the divswap compared to the fundamental value, the higher the risk perceived.**

---

[28] See chapters 5 and 6, "Dividend valuation model part 1, part 2"

It can be relevant to compare the value of fundamental analysis with the value of the divswaps to see how markets evaluate dividends. It can happen that the values are very different from each other, due to market expectations. **Those differences make some traders say that fundamental analysis is irrelevant since the quoted price is the price every trader uses, and is representative of both the value of the dividend and the risk it carries** (it carries the same information as using CDS spreads[29] to detect when a company is in trouble. Thus, according to some market makers, a standalone analysis of the value of the divswap is sufficient to assess the risks a company carries).

Impact of dividends amounts and dates on futures prices

We already presented some traits of the difference between futures and stocks/indexes. **The main difference between the two is that owners of futures contracts, whether on single stocks or on indexes, do not receive any dividends when stocks go ex-dividend.** The particularity of futures is that they do not embed the dividends that are to be paid (see the formula below).
That is why a trader will buy a future at a significant lower price than the spot, a price that must be computed.

To be more precise, here is how you evaluate the value of a future contract in indexes: (also work for single stocks).

$$\boxed{F = S \times e^{r \times T} - D}$$

With:
F: future contracts value
S: spot

[29] See chapter 3, "Index arbitrage: betting on the value with fundamental analysis", "Focus on dividend spiel"

D: dividends to be paid, in DIPs (index points)
r: interest rate annually
T: period of time considered.

Example:
We are the 1rst of January of the year XX.
The CAC 40 quotes at 3800 points.
Its companies are expected to pay 300 DIPs of dividends during the current year.
The interest rate for refinancing the operation is 75Bp.

What is today's value of the following contracts :
1) FUT DIV CAC 40 Dec-XX ?
2) FUT CAC 40 Dec-XX ?

Answers :
1) 300 points
2) 3528.607 points (3800*exp(0,5)-300)

And when the interest rates are at zero and the financing cost is very low, the whole difference of price between the future contract and the underlying basket are dividends. So if you are capable of pricing dividends better than your counterparts in other banks, your prices will be more accurate and potentially represent a better offer than your counterparts.

The different natures of dividends

Scrip versus cash

Paying a dividend in scrip consists in allowing shareholders to choose between receiving the dividend in cash and receiving the dividend in stocks. For example, if a company declares a dividend amount equaling 1:10th of the share's market price, for each existing ten shares a shareholder owns, he will receive whether one new share, or the market value of one share, in cash. The election ratio (the percentage of shareholders that chose to receive their dividends in stocks rather that in cash) depends on two factors that are in favor of the election of the dividend as stock:

- The **discount** is a bonus that the company gives to shareholders if they choose the stock. For example, for French stocks, the discount is comprised between 0 and 20%. A discount lowers the reference price[30] used to compute the dividend and thus increase the amount of shares to be emitted (shareholders who chose dividends in scrip will receive more shares. See example below);
- If there is a better **tax treatment** attached to the scrip alternative, shareholders will be more willing to choose the stock over the cash.

Number of existing shares	12 000 000 000
Total amount of dividends to be paid	250 000 000
The shareholders owns 10 shares	

Reference price	Number of shares
2,533	1,16
2,461	1,19
2,4	1,23
2,194	1,36

For a company, paying a scrip dividend has the advantage of retaining the capital in the company: before distributing the stock, the company proceeds to a capital increase by the amount of stocks that will be used as distribution. The amount of the capital increase is the nominal value of the share, (which can range from a few cents to several dozen euros, the minimum amount often being 1 cent of the currency), multiplied by the

30 Computed with the Volume-Weighted Average Price method.

number of shares emitted. There is no share premium since the stock is given for free as a dividend.

For a company, the advantage of paying a scrip dividend is weighted by two factors:

- The **percentage of election**, i.e. the percentage of shareholders that choose the stock over the cash. That amount can vary from 0% (every shareholder chose the cash) to 100% (every shareholder chose the stock). However, **this amount is determined by incentives** (discount and better tax treatment if dividends are elected in stocks, see above), **personal beliefs** (individual shareholders will receive the cash since they do not know they can elect in stocks, or they have a preference for cash) or **market habits** (traders will always choose the highest amount between cash and stock, on the last day of the election period);
- **Dilution**: each dividend elected in stock increases the number of a company's outstanding shares. Thus the dividend distribution per share in the following years, *ceteris paribus*, will be lower (**more stocks for an equal amount of dividend**) than the previous distribution. To keep up with a distribution, the bank will have to create even more stocks, etc. **In the end, even a stock dividend can become unsustainable**. For example, a dividend yield of 8% with an election ratio of 85% will lead to a 40%[31] increase in the number of stocks in just 5 years.

As a conclusion, a dividend paid in stocks following a scrip dividend option is **capital-conservative** for the part elected in stocks, since there is no cash outflow, and it can even increase the capital via the share nominal value. But this method is just a way to limit cash outflows, not a way to stop them, it is subject to several drawbacks such as **public incentives that might disappear** (the fiscal administration can decide to cancel fiscal gains on dividends elected in stocks), **randomness of the**

[31] Percentage of stock increase: (1+(0,08*0,85))^5-1

outcome (the percentage of election that can vary), **market conditions** (the cash value might suddenly be higher than the stock value) and **accelerated dilution**.

Quarterly, bi-annually, annually

Dividends can be paid at different frequency depending on companies policy. Their overall pattern is linked to the corporate calendar of the considered company: **dividends are generally announced during the financial results publication**. For example, a company will announce its annual results in February, and declare its annual dividend at the same time.

There are **three dividend patterns**[32]:

- Annually (once a year, announced at the Full Year results)
- Bi-annually (twice a year, generally announced at the half-year and the Full Year), or
- Quarterly (four times a year, announced during each quarterly result).

The dividend announced during Full Year results is called the **final dividend**, every other dividend is called an **interim dividend**. So **if a company pays four dividends a year, there will be three interim dividends and a final dividend**.

Warning: some company may cancel one interim dividend during a year of financial turmoil. The dividend must stay in your database, and the value be put at zero, since there still should be a dividend in the next following years.

Dividend dates

We already have evoked the calendar of a dividend: **each dividend paid**, whether by cash or by a scrip alternative (option

[32] A fourth pattern exists in more exotic countries: in Brazil for example, some companies are used to paying twelve dividends a year (one per month).

to elect the dividend in stock, often accompanied by incentives such as bonuses, see above), **has three dates that defines it**:

- The **record date**: it is the reference date to compute the ex-dividend date since there is an execution lag between the moment one buys a stock and one is the legal owner of it. In Europe, the settlement is made in T+2[33], meaning that the ex-dividend date is two business days after the record date. For example, on the T+2 system, if a dividend record date is on Wednesday, the ex-dividend is on Thursday[34]
- The **ex-dividend date**: it is the most important date and the only one that really matters. It is the date that is taken into account by indexes and contracts providers: **the contracts are quoted « cum-coupon » until the close of the day before the ex-dividend date**
- The **payment date**: it is the date when the dividend is delivered to the shareholder brokerage account, whether in cash or stock[35]

➢ Dividend calendar goes in this order: record date, ex-dividend date, payment date

Why is ex-dividend date so important?
If a futures contract, that expires on September, takes into account a dividend that detaches on the 10th, if the ex-date is postponed in November, the contract must no longer take the dividend into account. So the ex-dividend date is as important as the amount: **if the dividend date is mistakenly in the wrong month, the value of the dividend on the current month equals zero!**

Expiration of futures

[33] It was T+3 before October 2014. Other markets are willing to adopt the T+2 settlement in order to mitigate execution risks.
[34] And not Friday, as it is during the T+3 settlement. This example is taken from the example of British dividends. They used to have a record date on Wednesdays and an ex-dividend date on Fridays, and now the ex-date is on Thursdays. Be careful, financial website often states erroneous definitions.
[35] Dividends delivered in stocks are also said to be "paid".

Thus another important notion is the **expiration date of a future contract. A contract always expires on the third Friday of a month**. For example, the futures contracts for June-15 all expired on the 19th of June, 2015. **The most important dates are the four quarterly expiration dates**, those are the expirations that have most of the liquidity: March, June, September, December.

Ex-dividend date versus expiration date ?
To sum-up, if a dividend has an ex-dividend date before the expiration date of a contract, it will be priced within the contract until this date. But if the ex-dividend date is postponed from a monthly expiration to another (for example, a dividend that should have gone ex-dividend on the 19th of June, 2015, but was postponed to the 22nd of June, falls out of June expiration to enter...July expiration - and mechanically September expiry, which corresponds to the quarterly expiry). So if futures for the June expiry priced the dividend within and it went out, the whole dividend is lost for the trader. That is called a mispricing and it can be used to play strategies based on calendar (we will see that later).

- Expiration dates of contracts are always between the 15th and the 21st of the month (take a calendar and check it by yourself, you will understand better the mechanics of the expirations).

First day of the month	Date of the expiry
Monday	19th
Tuesday	18th
Wednesday	17th
Thursday	16th
Friday	15th
Saturday	21th
Sunday	20th

- If an ex-date of a dividend is between the 15th and the 21st of a month and you have not checked the monthly expiration, do it, there is a risk the dividend goes out of the monthly expiration (or enters)
- Analysts are watching closely months that have an expiration date near the 15th of the current month, it will be more likely that a dividend goes out of expiry
- The first thing to do when you start your job as an analyst is to print a calendar of the current year and the next two years, to highlight in fluorescent pen each third Friday of each month, so that you will have a fast access on the calendar when a dividend is announced, and will react quickly to notice every trader that the dividend goes out of (or gets in) an expiry

Ex-dividend date estimations and the importance of calendars

We saw that a mistake on ex-dividend dates can have larger consequences than a mistake on the amount, since errors on ex-dates can result in a 100 % loss. Moreover, if many companies pay a dividend once a year, many companies will pay a quarterly or biannually dividend, meaning that the estimation of the total dividend must then be split into one or three interim dividends and the final. In the end, the analyst must have the exact calendar for each company and flag the dividends that are at risk of going out of an expiration.

In order to estimate the ex-dividend date, you will find below the **main rules/patterns**. We provided some examples for each case. In any situation, the analysis of calendar and patterns will be the first step of dividend estimations. Be careful, those examples are general rules that can help you to find the ex-date, but in no way they are official rules. You will find more rules on the part on country specifics[36] (some countries have stricter rules on ex-dates).

Examples of patterns to estimate a dividend ex-date:

- The calendar of this year's dividend is the same as last year
- The ex-dividend date is (often/always) on the Xth day of the Yth week of the month of Z
- The ex-dividend date will be X working days after the dividend announcement (be sure to know how to use the function **networkdays()** on excel)
- The ex-dividend date will be X working days after the Annual General Meeting (It is the case in Germany)

Those rules are rarely official: companies use tricks when they decide the calendar of the year, they generally do not have much time and imagination to use random dates, they often use the same pattern as the previous years.

> ➢ The calendar can however be changed if it really is not convenient: an ex-date near a monthly expiration, during the winter vacations etc.

You may also find **two patterns for one company**: if one takes a fictive company: from 2001 and 2010, the dividend was detached two weeks after the AGM and starting from 2011, the delay shrank to one week. That often happens when major shareholders have preferences for the dividend payment and ask for a shift.

Moreover, it can happen that ex-dividend dates does not follow the pattern one year, and then goes back on track, due to shareholders demands, for fiscal reason: they will ask that the dividend is paid earlier versus the previous year just before a new fiscal law is passed. There is the subject in Spain notably.

---

[36] See chapter 4, "Dividends' specifics according to countries".

Focus: two examples of tricky changes of calendar.

The political factor

In this example, a shift by three weeks of the ex-dividend date happened, and not because of any matter on the dividends. This dividend was from a German company that had planned its AGM in an arena, like every other year, but the arena had been taken by the authorities to host refugees, so they had to postpone the date of the AGM. And since German dividends detach the day following the AGM, the ex-date was postponed by more than three weeks and went out of the monthly expiry.

The cultural factor

A dividend of a Russian stock quoted in USD was supposed to go ex-dividend on Friday the 4th of July. However, the depositary being in New York, its offices were closed. The actual ex-dividend date was postponed to Monday the 7th (see the chapter on specificities of eastern Europe).

Focus: fiscal year pattern versus calendar pattern.

When you compute the dividend for a current year, you make the reasoning based on earnings, meaning that the dividend announced during the Full Year results is paid after December (February or March generally). Thus the dividend does not detach during the calendar year you are studying.

Example: company A has announced on the 4th of February 2016 that it will pay its annual dividend for the fiscal year 2015 (that was closed on the 31st of December, 2015) on the 10th of February of 2016 and it will detach on the 12th of February, 2016.

So as for the example, the final dividend announced in February is paid on the results of the year 2015, but not paid in 2015. The dividend paid for 2015 was announced in February 2015 for the results of the year 2014.

And if a company had paid three interim dividends and a final dividend, the interim dividends would probably have been paid

in 2015 and the final in 2016. Making the Full Year dividend for 2015 to be composed of the three interim dividends paid in 2015 and the final paid in 2016. Not to be mixed with the calendar dividend for 2015, that is composed of the 2014 final dividend and the three interim dividends for 2015.
Be careful with that gymnastic!!

You still do not get the thing? Here is an example of the dividends of Total S.A.: we detailed the amount of dividend according to each type of year / the number of dividends paid:

Year	Calendar year	Fiscal year	Expiry year
2012	2,3 / 4	2,34 / 4	2,87 / 5
2013	2,36 / 4	2,38 / 4	2,36 / 4
2014	2,42 / 4	2,44 / 4	2,42 / 4
2015	2,44 / 4	2,44 / 4	1,83 / 3
2016	2,44 / 4	2,44 / 4	2,44 / 4

Rules of interim dividends versus final dividends

When the total amount of dividends that will be paid is computed, the analyst needs to split between the interim dividends and the final dividend in order to distinguish between the calendar annual dividend and fiscal year annual dividend (dividends paid out of a result of a specified year). And there can be as many split rules as companies: some will pay four equal installments, others will pay three equal interim dividends and a larger final etc.

Examples of rules that can apply:

- **Four equal installments**: example: Santander will pay for the 2015 results four installments of 5 euro cents making the total dividend paid on 2015 results to be 20 euro cents
- **Three equal installments and a slightly better fourth** (ex: HSBC will often do this strategy)

- **One interim and one final dividend**, the amount of the interim dividend being a fixed share of the final dividend of the previous year (example : the interim of 2015 represent 1/3 of the final of the final dividend of 2014) (example : beverage and tobacco companies)
- **One interim and one final dividend**, the interim dividend is half the final dividend;
- The total dividend for a fiscal year will **grow by X % each year**.

➢ Those rules are often official rules. They are disclosed in annual report, on Investors Relations statements, etc. Do not hesitate to pay a call to the Investors Relations offices too.

Warning :
We discussed above the difference between the "calendar aspects" of dividends and the "results aspect". An analyst must also be careful on the nature of the dividend: a company can pay an interim dividend in stocks, and every other dividend in cash. Or any other pattern it will want to do. There is no rule concerning the regularity in the nature of the dividend.

Regular dividends, special dividends.

A regular dividend is a dividend that is paid during **the normal process of production** of the company. The timing is always the same and the process follows the rules of financial disclosure as we explained in a previous part. Special dividends, however, just represent **an extra payback** to shareholders. This "gift" is not considered as part of the regular process of dividend payment, and thus is adjusted at 100% by indexes (not 100% for the EURO STOXX 50, since the tax treatment is not adjusted and represents percentages above 10%, depending on countries[37]).

Precision on the difference between regular and special

[37] See chapter 4: "Dividends' specifics according to countries" and chapter 5: "Dividend valuation model part 1: dividend amount".

dividends
We saw above that dividends were computed on regular items. To compute dividends, one must start with adjusted figures i.e. figures adjusted of exceptional financial items (one-off items). Exceptional items can most of the time be easily spotted: **a fine** (which is a cash outflow), **a provision** (which is not), a **large gain on an asset sale**, etc. **Be careful: external growth** (i.e. the company buys another company) **is not considered as exceptional**, and **thus any dividend cut can happen if the takeover is not financially sustainable of if there are covenants attached to the debt the company contracted for the operation.**

Special dividends paid in cash: spin off
The dividend which will be paid following a spin-off will be called "special dividend", it will not be taken into account for the computation of derivatives and thus is considered to be transparent from a derivatives point of view.

Dividend value until announcement and thereafter

Before a company announces its dividend (N.B.: most of the times, a company announces its dividends during results announcement), an estimation is made by the analyst using diverse methods that will be explained in the second part of this book[38]. Most of the time, several values are input in the databases used by traders: an analyst case based on analysts estimations with a base, a bear and a bull scenario, a divswap case and a Markit case.

N.B.: every market makers use Markit (now IHS-Markit) databases for a raw estimations of dividend amounts and patterns.

Until announced (and, from time to time, until effectively paid), dividends are considered to be theoretical, both in **existence** and

[38] See chapter 5:"Dividend valuation model part 1: dividend amount", chapter 6: "Dividend valuation model part 2: financial modeling"

in **amount**. When a company discloses a dividend amount and an ex-date, the dividend becomes official and its value is certain, and will not change[39].

When a dividend detaches, it also detaches in the index the stock is in. Its value in DIPs becomes fixed at the ex-date parameters (freefloat of companies, divisor, currency etc.) and dividends contracts do not incorporate the dividend any longer.

---

[39] Unless the AGM does not vote the amount the suggested by the board of directors, which never happens.

3

Strategies on dividends

Index arbitrage: betting on the value with fundamental analysis

One the works of traders, on an equity derivatives desk focused on indexes, is making money on arbitraging indexes. More precisely, they quote bids and asks on a product called EFP, or **Exchange of Futures for Physical**. An EFP is a product composed of a position on index futures and another inverse position on a basket that replicates the index.

For example, the trader will buy a basket on an index and sell the corresponding future. In order to do that, he will need to price the correct price for the future. As we have seen above, **index futures replicate the performance of the basket of stocks that replicates an index, without perceiving the dividends**. As such, the trader will evaluate the value **of the future contract based on the expected value of the dividends that will be paid**. But one must remember that the value taken for the dividends is not the nominal amount but the amount in Dividend Index Points (DIPs).

So in order to evaluate the index' future price, the analyst will compute the level of dividend in DIPs for each stock that composes the index. Then he will deduce the price of the future following the formula:

$$F = S \times e^{r \times T} - D$$

NB: one must also take into account the cost of financing, given by the loan desk in charge of borrowing and lending money to clients.

Focus on dividend *spiel*[40]:
It is not an arbitrage since you cannot speculate on the dividend itself and play its divswap. However **you can buy and sell divswaps** (it is an OTC transaction) if you notice **temporary market distortions** on the price. It is only speculation but traders have a long history of following the divswap price so they can notice any undervaluation.

The main undervaluation will happen for every company on a distressed sector even if all companies do not have the same profile of risk. For example, if the automotive sector is distressed due to one auto builder cheating on emission tests, every other automotive company will suffer from that event even if they are not concerned by the cheat. Then it's time to buy some cheap dividends!

[40] Spiel : German meaning "to play"

As I told the reader, **divswap price often work like CDS spreads**: when there is distress on a company (whether on the debt side or the business side), the CDS spreads increase and the divswap decreases. We however observed that CDS spreads increase's timing is at a delay versus the divswap price reduction's timing. The reason is understandable and is a sketch of the analysis that we will explain in part 2: while CDS spread only reacts to debt quality and sustainability, a divswap will embed many other events: global economic slowdown, currency inflation, exposure to distressed markets, production scandal, distress on debt, etc. for example, a pharmaceutical company that is not much levered but whose main product loses its FDA approval will certainly have its dividend at risk while its debt is not much more at risk.

Last but not least, let us all remember that a dividend is considered as part of equity and is thus paid after every other creditor is. **So the dividend is itself as risky as equity and must be apprehended as such by traders and investors**.

Ex-dividend dates shift due to a changing...

We already disclosed earlier that a change in the ex-dividend date is a very important event and can be disastrous, since the value of a futures contract depends on the dividends that will detach in the considered period. If a dividend ex-date is **postponed after the monthly expiry**, it is said to **go out of the monthly expiry**. If it is **advanced**, we say that **the dividend enters the monthly expiry**.

...calendar: change of expiry date

It is the most common reason why ex-dates change over the time. Here are a few examples:

- **If an ex-date is near an expiry**: every year it is the same date (for example 22/12) but each year, the monthly expiry date changes and thus **the dividend oscillates between "in the expiry" and "out of the expiry"**. The best example is when the ex-date of the dividend is around the December-expiry date. There are a lot of opportunities in this configuration (see Total S.A. dividend).

  - On sub-example of the event date impact on the dividends is for German stocks. There is one notable example in which two subsidiaries of a global group are so large that they are quoted on the same index. Their AGM date is separated by one day. In 2014, the AGM of the former was on a Thursday, and the AGM of the latter was on the Friday of the monthly expiry. So the two dividends were not in the same monthly expiry. The previous year had not met this pattern, so it was not expected to happen. However, the case quite uncommon, and we only have one example of company (Fresenius SE and Fresenius AG) in mind. This type of events happens much more frequently for American Depositary Receipts (see part on Eastern Europe indexes).

- **Change of event date that postpones the ex-dividend date**: for example if a company choses to delay a results announcement by two months, there is a huge probability that the dividend will be postponed by two months. It can happen when there are mergers and acquisitions, so that the companies have the same calendar when they merge. Another example is when the Annual General Meeting/Results announcement is postponed, so is often the ex-dividend date.
- **Change of settlements rules** (no occurrence observed): when the settlements rules came from a T+3 to a T+2 settlement delay (there was to be two days between the ex-dividend date and the record date, now one), the delay between the ex-dividend date and the record date was shortened by one day. In some configurations, when the rule was implemented, there could have been a shift in the ex-dividend date that could have presented an arbitrage opportunity.

- **There is no rule to determine future monthly expiry dates knowing the current month expiry date**. For example, the pattern of monthly expiries in 2015 was (first figure is January 2015 expiry, etc.): 16, 20, 20, 17, 15, 19, 17, 21, 18, 16, 20, 18.

Focus on the Dec-14 dividend of Total S.A.

There was an event in 2014 on the Total S.A. dividend calendar, that created an investment opportunity. The calendar had not been published yet, and the dividend that would go ex-dividend in 2015 was expect to be in Dec-15 expiry (before 18/12), like the previous year. Traders priced Total S.A. dividend in Dec-15 expiry, but some of them noticed there was a risk that the dividend would go out of Dec-15 expiry. It is interesting to note that Total S.A. has one of the largest market capitalizations in Europe, so its weight in the EURO STOXX 50 and CAC is significant, and its divswap is very liquid.

Some traders decided to play the shift of ex-date of Total. It was all the more interesting since the market priced the dividend **within** Dec-15 expiry. **The price of buying dividend out of Dec-15 expiry was thus at nearly zero**. Buying the dividend for jan-16 expiry was thus comparable to a call option at zero cost (a free call). It was costless to play the dividend going out of Dec-15 expiry with potential large gain. If the dividend ex-date was eventually within Dec-15 expiry, the loss would have been limited to the amount of the "call" (= very little amount).

Total S.A. eventually announced the calendar and the dividend went out of Dec-15 expiry. A bunch of traders made large gains out of it.

One idea of strategy would be to play every dividend that has a slight risk of going out an expiry and backtest this strategy's profitability.

...nature of the dividend: scrip versus cash

One well known reason an ex-dividend date could be advanced in time is when a stock used to pay a dividend in cash and then starts paying a scrip. In effect, **when a company changes the nature of its dividend from cash to scrip, it will desire to preserve the payment date of the dividend**. Since the scrip dividend payment requires several steps in order to be computed, **the ex-dividend date must be earlier than when the dividend was paid in cash**.

To be more precise, **the delay is around 20 working days**, which corresponds to the period during which the value of the dividend paid in stock is computed.

This can be interesting if the ex-date of a cash dividend is within a quarterly expiry and it starts paying a scrip dividend. We saw one example with Publicis. For the dividend paid in June 2014, everyone expected a cash dividend to be paid, so the ex-date was expected to be within the same expiry as the previous years (to be more precise, **the previous year was already a scrip dividend but the markets expected this scrip to be a one-off**). A call to the IR[41] told me that this year would also be a scrip, despite what markets priced. This was another example of free call (at the condition that Publicis divswap existed).

...fiscal policy

In this short example, as per 2015, there was an ongoing fiscal reform on the dividend in Spain. So each time companies fear that the government is about to pass such a law, they advanced their ex-dividend date and payment date to the month before the law is due, so that shareholders are not affected for the next dividend in case the law is passed. However it has been several years that such law was about to be passed and there is still no law...

---

[41] Investors Relations

Dividend index valuation: the interest of building bottom-ups

You were already told a little bit about bottom-ups, which are Excel files that compute each dividend in **Dividend Index Points**, with several cases, and thus can evaluate the total of DIPs per year that detach from the index. There are **two types of bottom-ups**: the **consolidated** ones (each line represents a company, the DIPs computed for each company is the sum of every dividend the company pays, in DIPs) and the **detailed** ones (same principle as the consolidated one, except it allows the reader to have to roadmap of every dividend to be paid).

The consolidated bottom-up has the advantage to be readable, and it is the occasion to put several cases alongside. However it is very complicated to build since you must use advanced Excel formulas to compute sums of dividends in DIPs (that are a product of the amount in currency by the ratio weight of the stock/divisor). Moreover, you must distinguish between dividends that will detach in the future and those that have already been detached, and when every dividend is consolidated for each stock, it can become tricky. It requires strong knowledge and much care in building those models for it can contain many hidden errors.

The detailed bottom-up is much simpler: there is **a line for each dividend**. So if you sort the Excel file by ex-date, you get a calendar of every dividend that will detach. You must update this calendar when the dates and amounts are published, but you get instant values on the dividend that already have detached and the ones that will detach in the future. Moreover it enables the analyst to do some scenarios on the amount/ ex-date of future dividends.

Focus on EMTN structuration

Bottom-ups are very useful to price the level of expected DIPs in an index, and compare it to a dividend index future. If the price of a dividend index future is much lower than the value of the bottom up (that evaluates your expectations in terms of dividends to be paid), there may be a buying opportunity. However this move is not risk free since the dividend index future reflects the market expectations of dividend values, and a low level can be the proof that markets expect major cuts.

If the value of the total DIPs computed is different from the dividend index value by a large amount, it can be a good tool to valuate dividends that are not priced in the markets. By deducing the dividends that have a quoted divswap or by making assumptions on the likeability of a cut, you can evaluate the level of dividend indexes (in DIPs). For example, if you remove the amount of quoted divswap and make very conservative assumptions of the other dividends to be paid, and still find a price way above the index value, it is a good "buy" signal.

With such a "buy" signal, a trader can propose to its clients to buy the level of dividends now (under the shell of an EMTN), which are valued at market price, in the hopes that it will reach the value priced by the bottom-up.

Example:
An index is composed of 5 stocks (A, B, C, D, E) that pay dividends. Below is a table with the amount of dividends and the stock freefloat.

Hypothesis:
The currency is the euro
Today is the 01/01/XX
The reference price at the creation of the index: 1000
Cap of capitalization: there is a cap for stock A of 0.50
See formula in chapter 2 for the computation
Divisor: 2048
Dividend Index quoted price: 520
The nominal of a contract: 1.000

Stock name	Estimated Dividend	Freefloat	Quoted Divswap, if any
A	0,3	1.5 Bn	0,25
B	1	300m	0,85
C	5	150m	-
D	1,1	100m	-
E	2	100m	-

1) compute the estimated DIPs that are to detach in the Index, based on the estimated dividend
2) compute the estimated DIPs that are to detach in the index, based on quoted divswaps
3) compute the gains for the following strategy:

- Buy 1 contract of the Dividend Index on 01/01/XX
- Close the position on 31/12/XX
- Every estimations of dividends proved correct

Answers:
1) Estimated DIPS: 737.2
2) Estimated DIPs with divswaps: 698.83
3) profit: 217,200 euros ((737.2-520)*1000)

Index recomposition arbitrage and divisor estimation

There are two well-known arbitrages attached to **index recomposition** (when a stock goes out of an index and another enters the index, also called **index rebalancing**). In order to better understand those arbitrages, we suggest you read a short description of how market recompositions work[42].

Stock arbitrage

The first arbitrage on corporate action **is on stocks** that will go out or enter the recomposed index. During the two months

[42] The chapter 5, "Aggregate indicators: stock indices", in "The Complete Arbitrage Deskbook", by Stéphane Reverre is a must-read.

preceding the index recomposition, stocks with the lowest capitalization will be scrutinized in order to see if they are eligible for an exit of the index. If so, there also will be a stock that will enter the index. There can be more than one stock to go out at each index recomposition.

On the day the recomposition is officially announced, the stock to go out will face a push to get out and the stock to get in will get a lift. This is due to fund managers who must replicate indexes and thus integrate the recomposition when it is announced. Other market participants (especially delta one desks and hedge funds) can anticipate this shift in stock value to play a long/short strategy: **you are long from the stock(s) you expect to enter, and you get short from the stock(s) you expect to go out**.

If there are stocks eligible for an exit (roughly if their market capitalization is too low[43]), so is one stock eligible to integrate the index. There are several rules to follow (some can be very tricky), but in the end you can **build a selection list of eligible stocks to go in and out**. You now can play the stock(s) you expect to go out and the stock(s) you expect to get in.

Index recompositions occur once a year in September (the cut-off date of the review is the last trading day of august). The recomposition is not automatic, and it can happen that no stocks is going out.

Dividend arbitrage

The second arbitrage is on dividends : when there is an index recomposition, the divisor of the index will change : it will go down with the capitalization of the stock that goes out and go up with the capitalization of the stock that gets in. Two strengths will then apply (ceteris paribus):

- **The yield** : if a low yielder goes out and is replaced by a high yielder, the total value of the dividend index will increase (example: a company who pays a dividend that

[43] The rules are disclosed on STOXX website. See Appendix 2.

yields 5,5% replaces a company that yields 1,1%, it will relute the dividend index);

- **The market capitalization**: if a stock with a small market capitalization goes out and is replaced by a larger market cap, the divisor will increase and the level of the index will decrease.

Moreover, there is a rule that stipulates that the market value at the close of the index before the index recomposition must equal the value of the index at the opening after the recomposition. So the index provider will adjust the value of the divisor so that the index value stays the same. What will eventually change is the dividend index value (and that can be arbitrated) since the divisor and dividend value will change (see reasoning above).

As a conclusion, if you have an estimation of the dividend of the potential stocks that would enter the index, you can make assumptions on the divisor and compute the expected value of the dividend index future. You can now arbitrate it.

Focus: computation of the index divisor <u>before</u> a recomposition is announced.
It is impossible to compute from scratch the divisor of an index since it is not a linear sum of the capitalizations of the stocks that compose it. However you can approximate the value of the index after a recomposition, by constructing the index as it will be.
First Step: you remove the stock that should go out and incorporate the stock that should enter the index (according to your estimations). With the freefloat capitalization of those stocks, and the divisor of today, you can compute the value of the index today.
Second step: you then resolve a simple equation: the value of the index you computed must equal the value of the index today. One only needs to adjust the value of the divisor. You will have to repeat the operation every day (since the new entrants, the value of every freefloat can change rapidly, and corporate actions modify the value of the divisor) to provide an accurate

value of the divisor.

The tricky part is to get the freefloat of the new entrants. This information is given by the index providers: for the EURO STOXX 50 recomposition, you can have the freefloat of every larger company in Europe by checking the EURO STOXX 600. A few weeks before recomposition, STOXX will publish a short list for index recomposition with the definitive freefloat (check the calendar on their website. For European indexes, the index provider is STOXX and the website is https:// www.stoxx.com/).

4

Dividends' specifics according to countries

Focus on Western European markets

Euronext

Indexes[44]:

- CAC 40 (Cotation Assistée en Continu, France, 40 stocks, WHT : 30%[45])
- BEL20 (Belgium, 20 stocks, WHT: 27%)
- PSI-20 (Portuguese stock Index, Portugal, 20 stocks, WHT: 25%/35%)

---

44 Please note that the names of the indexes may be different from one to another. Some have space between their names and the figures, other do not.

45 Figures for 2016, idem for every following country. Source: Deloitte, "Withholding Tax Rates 2016".

- AEX (Amsterdam Exchange, the Netherlands 25 stocks, WHT: 15%/25%)

Spain: scrips and tax incentives

Index: IBEX 35 (Ìndice Bursàtil Español, 35 stocks). Regulator: CNMV. WHT: 19%.

We discussed above the interest of paying a scrip dividend (a dividend with the option to elect the dividend in stocks instead of cash) for companies. In Spain, scrip dividends are an institution: most companies propose their dividend as scrips, and provide great details on how they compute the dividends (**see Appendix 2**). It is also the country with **highest election ratio** (often above 80%) since **scrip dividends are not taxed** (versus 19% for cash dividends).

However, the problem of dilution in companies paying a scrip dividend is so large that it urged the Spanish government to take actions by passing laws in order to limit the payment of scrip dividends. Eventually, some banks stopped paying dividend since they could not pay cash dividends in the stead of cash dividends. **That is why the weakest Spanish banks have an erratic pattern of dividend payments**, some of them stopping to pay and then resuming a few months/years later.

There is a pattern of scrip for Spanish stocks that is always the same. Most companies respect this procedure (see **Appendix 2**).

NB: for spanish scrips: ex-date = payment date .

Italy: dividend go ex-coupon on Mondays

Index: FTMIB (Footsie MIB, Milano Italia Borsa, 40 stocks). Regulator: CONSOB. WHT: 26%.

The ex-dividend date for Italian stock is peculiar: when a dividend is announced, its ex-dividend date is the Monday following the monthly expiry. For example, if a company announced its dividend on the 6th of January 2015, its ex-dividend date was most likely on Monday the 19th.

Another rule: contrary to the other countries, results in Italy **are not necessarily published before market opening or after market close** but most often during the day. When major Italian companies announce their results, you have to skip lunch!

British DRIPs: no incentives to elect the stock

Index: FTSE 100 (Footsie 100, 100 stocks). Regulator: FCA.

DRIPs, or Dividend Re-Investment Plans are a form of scrip used by British companies: it consists in the same thing as a scrip dividend (it allows investors to "reinvest" their dividends in the index by choosing the stocks).

But contrary to European scrips, there is no discount attached to DRIPs. That is why DRIPs are never elected as dividends. In a previous study, I estimated that 5% of Royal Dutch Shell and 20% of BP dividends were elected as stocks in 2014, while 85% of Repsol dividends and Total S.A. dividends were elected as stocks.

That is why British companies do not have the same leverage to reduce the cash outflow when paying dividends, as European companies do. That is an important criteria of analysis, especially when the FTSE100 hosts the largest **banking group** in the world (HSBC), two of the largest integrated oil and gas (Royal Dutch Shell and BP), the four largest **mining companies** (BHP Billiton, Rio Tinto, Anglo-American and Glencore), and **those three sectors are the largest yielders of the index**.

Swiss capital contribution reserves

Index: SMI (Swiss Market Index, 20 stocks). Regulator: FINMA. WHT: 35%.

Swiss dividends have a specificity that must be noted. Many of them[46] come from what is called a **capital contribution reserves** (also called: additional paid in capital, supplementary capital, etc.) which is considered as a Capital Return (abbreviation on Bloomberg: CR). It is a dividend paid with special reserves ("capital contribution reserves") considered as own capital and **that is tax free**. It is the same as regular dividends paid on the net income attributable to shareholders, but instead of decreasing the capital added by retained earnings, **it decreases a reserve that was constituted during a determined period of time** (from 2008 to 2011) for giving incentives to invest in the Swiss stock market. This advantage was frozen by federal fiscal authorities (in 2011), however Swiss authorities still have a grip on those reserves since they validate their lawfulness and amount each year (they validate the maximum reserves that can be used to pay dividends. We do not have any precedent of fiscal authorities blocking the distribution of dividend out of those special reserves).

The specificity of those reserves is that they are of a fixed amount from 2011 and **can only be depleted**. They cannot be increased by any means but proceeding to a capital increase and attributing the **nominal value** of the shares emitted to the special reserves. Nominal value is often very low (it can be as low as one cent) and that amount is not significant for dividend payment.

If each year a dividend is paid out of those reserves, they are depleted each year. **One can thus compute the number of years remaining before those reserves are entirely depleted**, by estimating the average dividend to be paid in the following years (one can built best/worst cases), and multiply this value by the number of stocks that receive dividends. **When only a few years remain** (less than 3), it becomes interesting to compute the available reserves, since not every trader will do so and there may be some arbitrage opportunities.

---

[46] ABB, Actelion, Adecco, Credit Suisse, Givaudan, LafargeHolcim, SwissRe, Transocean, UBS, Zurich Re

One must take into account the potential capital increase preceding the payment of dividends: if a company makes a capital increase of 10% and then pays its annual dividends, the new shares will be eligible to receive the dividends paid out of capital contribution reserves.

Last but not least, **only cash dividends can be paid out of capital contribution reserves**. Scrip dividends elected in stocks and stocks distribution (free share allocation as explained in a part before) are also eligible to tax free distribution but do not deplete those reserves (but for their nominal value). In our opinion, **this is a tax loophole** since it will cost the tax payer a large amount of money since it can last forever and the fiscal administration will not perceive any money on those allocations.

- **It is not mandatory to pay dividends out of capital contribution reserves** if a company has some. The distribution of those reserves is discretionary and companies can pay a mix (half taxable, half tax free) or possibly a 100% taxable dividend.
- **There is absolutely nothing else to do than paying tax-free dividends with those reserves**. That is why companies tend to deplete those reserves **as fast as they can** before fiscal rules change.

Name	BBG code	Theoretical stock at Dec-15 in mCHF	Par value of the share, in CHF
ABB	ABBN	0	0,86
Actelion	ACTN	417,83	
Adecco	ADEN	142,93	1,0
Credit Suisse	CSGN	16.528	

Givaudan	GIVN	401,5	10,0
Holcim[47]	HOLN	5.293,37	
Swiss Re	SREN	0	0,01
Transocean	RIGN	8.159,07	15
UBS	UBSN	36.548	0,10
Zurich Re	ZURN	3.426,52	0,01

Theoretical value for Dec-15 Swiss additional paid-in capital reserves.

Another way of paying tax-free dividends: share nominal reduction

Some companies have emitted stocks with a nominal value higher than the minimum allowed (0.01 CHF). The fiscal administration of Switzerland allows companies to pay a tax-free dividend by reducing the nominal value of their shares. When doing that, the nominal value is reduced by the amount of dividend paid, until it reaches the minimum value allowed. **Companies will most likely use this technique if they already pay a dividend out of capital contribution reserve, in order to expand as much as possible the tax-free dividends program.** When they are about to run out of nominal to attribute as dividend, they pay a part taxed and a part tax-free dividend.

Focus on emerging markets: BRICs, Eastern Europe

In Brazil, ten or more interim dividends are paid

Brazilian companies are used to paying a large number of interim dividends. It is often that you will see nine interim dividends and one final. This does not represent any particular problem, but be careful on your bottom-up to be sure to have every dividend, as one can easily be forgotten. Some of them are special dividends

[47] Now, LafargeHolcim. The stock of additional paid-in capital has been integrated in the new company balance sheet, and will be used as Holcim did before.

that are adjusted and whose value in the bottom-up, shall we say it again, is null. Be careful and spot them.

WHT: 0%.

Presentations of Eastern Europe countries: Poland, Russia

- **Indexes: WIG 20, CECE, RDX**

In this short part, we sum up some characteristics of Eastern European dividends. They are not very liquid markets and the markets participants on those indexes are a few. Those markets often face the issue of devaluation of the currencies they are labeled in: when you trade stocks and dividends in a very volatile currency, you end up trading the currency itself rather than the amount of the dividend (a 20 % dividend cut is nothing if the currency loses 50 % of its value).

We will study three indexes : the polish index (WIG20), the eastern European index (CECE EUR[48]) that quotes stocks from Poland, Hungary, Czech Republic, and the RDX which consists of Russian stocks[49] traded in New-York.

Specificities of those indexes

a. On the RDX

- **Stocks quoted on the RDX are not quoted with a parity of 1:1 versus the MICEX**. They are American Depositary Receipts (ADR) that have a parity that can go from 1:40 to 1:2000. Be careful when you compute the levels of DIPs for the RDX: if a Russian company pays a 4 RUB dividend

[48] Index from the Wiener Börse.

[49] Normally traded on the MICEX)

and its parity with ADRs is 1:40, it will be as if this ADR paid a RUB 160 dividend!

- In your bottom-up, you obviously must enter **the currency exchange rate** (USD/RUB) as a variable since it **is very volatile**
- There is **no concept of ex-dividend date or payment date for Russian stocks**: Russian companies disclose the record dates and then the ex-dividend dates must be deduced from those. Ex-dividend dates are generally 10 business days after the record date
- **Dividends are paid according to Russian laws but depositaries follows US laws.** If the ex-dividend date ends-up on a vacation day in the US, the ex-dividend date will be postponed to the following business day. For example, if a record date is the 2nd of July (on a Wednesday), the ex-dividend date will not be Friday the fourth of July but Monday the 7th...[50]
- **In the past, some dividends could go ex-div and then be cancelled or modified (in amount[51])**: there was an old rule of ex-dividend date saying that the dividend would go ex on a date announced by the company, but not necessarily after the dividend is voted by the Annual General Meeting. So there could be the interesting situation in which the amount was reduced or the dividend was cut due to the non-approval of the dividend by the AGM (or a phone call by the local authorities saying the dividend was tool low or too high[52]).

WHT: 15%.

---

[50] In case you are wondering, it happened in July 2014 on a Russian stock.

[51] This rule was cancelled in early 2010's.

[52] Too low when the government has stocks in the company, too high when the largest shareholder is a foreign (meaning: American or European) company.

b. On the CECE EUR

The CECE is the eastern European index that is comprised of Polish, Hungarian and Czech stocks[53], and is quoted is Austria.

N.B.: Polish stocks both quoted on the WIG 20 and on the CECE will see their interim dividends be adjusted at a 100% on the CECE but not adjusted on the WIG.

WHT: 19% (Poland), 0% (Hungary), 15%/35% (Czech Republik), Austria (27.5%).

Conclusion of chapter 4

Market announcement of dividends in the morning

The aim of the rules we presented is to build a bottom-up, which is used in the pricing of an equity derivative called an EFP (**Exchange of Futures for Physical**). As we already said, when building a bottom-up and pricing an EFP, the analyst must follow day-after-day the stocks that are announced and stocks that go ex-dividend, until the next expiry.

For that reason, the pricing tool, whether it is a database on a software or an excel file, must take into account:

- The number of DIPs that have not detached yet in the index, up to the followed expiry;
- The day-to-day dividend announcement in order to compute the most precise number of DIPs that remain to be announced/to detach.

That is why it is also very important to build a calendar of every dividend announcement to come. Large trading desks build their own calendars with tools like Bloomberg, Markit and also by hands (it is the most fastidious job yet the most effective to have a precise calendar). When the analyst arrives at his desk

53 Not every stock of a country is quoted on the CECE and not every stock quoted on the CECE is quoted in every country).

in the morning, he will be responsible for checking any dividend announcement and market moving news. According to the desk's internal strategies, the analyst will be in charge of the notification of any news, whether good or bad, and potentially to compute the impact of the dividend announcement on the PnL[54]. He will also have to make a quick analysis on the results announcements, if he thinks it may have an impact on the dividend. The most difficult period of the year is the full year results, between mid-January and mid-March, when every large company announces its results and a dividend: there can be ten or fifteen companies that announce on a single day. Notably, Thursdays are the busiest day of the week.

[54] Profit and Loss

5 Dividend valuation model part 1: dividend amount

Introduction

Dividends are paid out of net income attributable to shareholders, with cash the company has on its balance sheet. So, two conditions must be met in order for a company to pay a dividend: there must be enough results and enough cash. But before any financial consideration is taken into account, the amount of the **expected** dividend to be paid must be computed. Only after this step (or in parallel), the analyst will study the financials to check if the studied company meets the two conditions (enough results, enough cash).

This chapter introduces to you the first part of the **dividend valuation model**, which is called the computation of the expected amount to be paid.

If you study a balance sheet, it should look like something like:

Assets	**Liabilities**
Properties, plants and equipment	Equity
Cash and other financial assets	Net income
Working capital	Financial Debt
Total Assets	**Total Liabilities**

As it is understandable, paying a dividend in cash will decrease the assets (cash items) and the liabilities accounts (net income attributable to shareholders). For dividends paid in stocks, the net income will decrease by the nominal value of the stock while the equity will increase for the same amount. So paying a dividend in stocks is costless for a company, however there are several drawbacks and it is not always a possibility[55].

Secondly, the cash condition is more imperative than results (except for scrips). **Under the assumption that the company cannot (and will not) increase its debt to pay dividend**, if a company has not enough cash on its balance sheets, it will not be able to pay a cash dividend. Should it be impossible for the company to pay a scrip dividend (example: UK drips that are never elected as stocks), the company will have de facto to cut its dividend by the amount in excess of what it owns. Companies that have more flexibility of their scrip dividend program will be less likely to cut their dividends.

---

[55] Drawbacks: it creates dilution. Moreover, scrip dividend program are not always available for the companies.

Different values

When valuating an EFP (=computing the DIPs that have not detached in the index yet), the analyst will have to take several cases in order to provide an **interval of confidence**. The basic computations are:

- **A base scenario**: the dividend estimation is the most credible estimate by the analyst (with a probability);
- **A bear scenario**: the most conservative estimation (with a probability)
- **A bull scenario** : the most optimistic estimation (with a probability),
- **An average scenario**: the average of the base, bull and bear scenario weighted by their respective probability;
- **A divswap case**: when available, the analyst will replace the nominal estimated value of the dividend by the value of its divswap, when it is quoted. For the stocks that do not have a quoted divswap, use the Markit case;
- **A Markit case**: use the estimations made by Markit. Every trader uses Markit estimations since it is easy to handle, there are up-to-date and Markit analysts are dedicated to estimating dividends. Warning: Markit cases are overestimated by large amount, so it is possible that you have to discount the amount by 10% or 20%. There is also a problem on British and US stocks: you have to compute the net amount of the dividend since the amount is given gross (you multiply by 90% to have the dividend after tax since **British and US dividends are computed tax-free**).

➢ The sum of the probability of **the base, the bull and the bear scenario must be equal to 1**.

Taxation

When estimating the dividend amount, one always computes the gross amount. When the dividends are announced, companies always announce the gross amount. When paid, the net amount is paid to the shareholder while there is a tax retained that goes to the state where the dividend is paid.

Moreover, the indexes adjust the dividend by its gross amount (not every index do, some of them adjust the dividend by the net amount) that is why the fiscal consideration must not be taken when computing the dividends. And last but not least, equity derivatives desks are subject to « **market tax rate** » that is different from the tax rate of individual shareholders. The only way to check the market rate is to ask the traders that will know or ask their Back Office / Depositary.

The tax on dividends is called « withholding tax » (abbreviated by « WHT »), the tax is usually paid by shareholders but it is levied by the depositary of the dividends.

- We already saw that some Swiss dividends were tax free and thus the WHT is zero
- Some companies pays the WHT of their announced dividends, so that the shareholders receive 100 % of the amount announced (example : Philips)
- **Some companies have a hybrid taxation system**: this is the case for Real Estates Investments companies, where some parts of the dividend can be exonerated from tax for it is produce by real estate activities (the dividend is issued from the "SIIC" regime[56]). For example, one part of Unibail Rodamco dividend is paid out of real estate entity and thus can be tax free according to a law. The remaining part is 100 % taxable
- There is no withholding tax on British stocks

Full year 2013 Unibail-Rodamco dividend announcement:

[56] SIIC means « Sociétés d'Investissement Immobilier Cotées » (french for Real-Estate Investment Listed Company)

> Shareholders approved the Company's annual accounts for the financial year 2013 and resolved to distribute a dividend of **€8.90 per share**, comprising:
>
> - €3.90 per share in cash paid from the Group's tax exempt real estate activities (dividend issued from the "SIIC" regime) and,
> - €5.00 per share in cash paid from the Group's non-tax exempt activities (dividend not issued from the "SIIC" regime)
>
> The dividend will be paid on May 15, 2014. The ex-dividend date is May 12, 2014.

- ➢ Tax rules can vary from time to time, according to countries, companies, politics, etc. A regular review of the taxation systems is required.

Last but not least, dividends are quoted in 100 % perceived by the shareholders, so when a trader announces that he « will receive 85 », it means that he will receive 85 % of the dividends announced.

Table: withholding tax on dividends, at the 1rst of January 2016[57]*.*

Country	Tax rate	Comment
Austria	27,5%	
Belgium	27,0%	
Brazil	0,0%	
Canada	25,0%	
Czech Republik	15%/35%	
France	30,0%	
Germany	25,0%	
Hungary	0,0%	
Ireland	0%/20%	Subject to EU directive
Italy	26,0%	
Netherlands	0%/15%	Subject to EU directive
Poland	19,0%	
Portugal	25%/35%	35% rate apply to resident of tax haven jurisdictions
Russia	15,0%	
Spain	19,0%	
Switzerland	35,0%	
UK	0,0%	All dividends are subject to a 10% tax paid before the dividend payment
USA	30,0%	

Pattern-based analysis

The pattern-based analysis is the study of dividends from a corporate history point-of-view and not a market point of view: our aim will be to estimate the amount of dividends with the payment pattern of a company.

[57] Source: Deloitte, Withholding Tax Rates, 2016.

Here are the main criteria to assess the amount of dividends to be paid.

Some companies announce their policy by disclosing:

- **The historical pattern**:
    - The dividend grows X% per year, so this year is expected to be at a X% growth
    - The company pays a dividend within a cycle: steady growth in the first years, dramatic increase in the last years before a merger or a buy-out. So continues the cycle
    - The interim dividend is half the final of the previous year
- **The payout ratio**: companies will disclose past payouts and target payouts. The payout ratio is applied on the net income attributable to shareholders. This method is the most commonly used since it is the easiest. It is very useful when the company has a target payout ratio or even directly communicates its expected payout[58] ratio. However it has little to no sense to use the historical payout ratio to compute the forecasted dividend, if the company does not have a target payout ratio. It can be used to have another view on the estimation but cannot ever replace a deeper analysis[59]
- **The cash capacity**: we will have a dedicated part on the cash generation analysis. The theory is simple: the company must manage its cash in order to afford paying dividends

[58] The formula is : dividend per share = (payout ratio x net income attributable to shareholders)/number of outstanding shares

[59] The problem with the payout ratio is that it is too much rigid. When declaring a dividend, companies will prefer to adjust the payout ratio rather than the amount. For example, a target of 40 % payout can lead to an effective payout of 35 % (if the results are better than expected) or 45 % (if they are lower)...

- **Other methods disclosed by companies also exist**: some companies will highlight that the decision of paying a dividend is a combination of net income/adjusted net income/recurring net income, capital expenditure, indebtedness, external growth. When disclosed, it is a sign that things are turning sour. In effect, computing a dividend and using elements other than cost/net income means that there may not be enough cash and/or net income.

You will find in **Appendix 6** some examples of historical dividend payments to see the growth/the regularity of them.

The divswaps

As we already saw, some people will argue that **divswaps are the best estimates of the value of a dividend** since it embeds an **intrinsic value** (based on the results of the company), a **time value** (the divswap value changes over time over the increase/decrease of results versus expectations) and a **risk value** (the divswap is a good indicator of a distressed company since it has a tendency to drop when there is a stress on the company).

The limits of this analysis are:

- The divswap does not communicate on the business plan of the company, its strengths and weaknesses, its management, its debt situation (it only does when it is already too late), etc.
- Not every company, even from the largest index, have a quoted divswap
- And, when quoted, a divswap is not necessarily very liquid and its price can be not continuous. In these situations, it is most appreciable to have a fundamental analysis to rely on, when assessing a dividend's value.

➢ **Using a divswap to evaluate a dividend is like using the market capitalization of a company to assess its**

value. It is not fundamentally flawed, but if an analyst does that, he will be fired immediately!

Conclusion

Other analysis techniques based on calendar, counterparts practices and historical patterns, are used to assess a dividend value, but more on the aspect of disruption than on the amount itself:

- Change of dividend pattern
- Risk of dividend cut
- Change of nature : scrip versus cash

We already talked about it earlier in this book, but **those parameters are very important since they are not continuous**: in a troubled company, a dividend value will oscillate between a positive value and zero without any continuity.

We can however use those **three parameters** (ie : risk on the pattern, risk of a cut and risk of change in nature) to assess the risk embedded to the **broad sector** to which a company belongs. For example, integrated oil and gas companies will have the tendency to pay four installments instead of one, due to the cyclicality of the cash-flows. Thus if an oil and gas company still pays one dividend a year, there is a probability that **it will eventually** go to a four-installment pattern. On the same principle, if a mining company cuts its dividend due to a commodity rout, it is expectable that **other will follow**. We can expand this reasoning with scrip dividend programs: a company will most likely start paying a scrip (or a cash if it already pays a scrip) if companies from its sector does the same.

Overall, **the financial health of sectors in general is often key determinants in the dividend policy of the companies that compose those sectors**. That is why dividend analysis can be performed for each company but analysts also regularly publish sectorial reports.

6

Dividend valuation model part 2: financial modeling

Introduction

As we have already seen, there are several tools to assess the value of a dividend, the most common one being the use of the payout ratio. However we also saw that the capacity of the company to generate **net income is one condition** out of two, **the second one being to have enough cash** on its balance sheet to do so.

We will also see a third condition that applies to financial institution: more than generating a result and enough cash,

those institutions must also be allowed to pay dividends. We will see that financial regulation can be a huge deterrent in this process.

This chapter details the second part of the **dividend valuation model**, e.g. the use of financial analysis to **check that the company has the financial means to pay dividends**, and if necessary, correct the amount computed during the first part (reduce the amount if the company cannot afford a dividend as computed before, or increase the amount of the dividend, including adding a dividend for special one-off items).

The FCFF model: the basis

The reader of this paper will probably be acquainted to **Free Cash-flow to the Firm** models (**FCFF**), or any other Free Cash-flow models such as the discounted free cash-flow used in evaluating a company. The principle is simple: **a company will pay its dividends on the free cash flow it generates**. With its cash, it will have to pay every other stakeholder and the remnants will go to the shareholders.

The basic model will be:

1 – Computing the FCFF with the formula: **FCFF: CFO**[60] **– CAPEX**[61]
2 – Building the financial model derived from the net debt (also called "**cash from financing activities**")
3 – Assessing other risks attached to a company production cycle and indebtedness: financial covenants, the ability to control CAPEX, the currency of its production cycle etc.

You can ask yourself why we decided to us the FCFF model (by separating the Free Cash-flow and the net debt variation) and

---

[60] CFO = Cash-flows from operation
[61] CAPEX = Capital Expenditure = investment

why we did not use the Free Cash-flow the Equity model directly. As a reminder:

$$FCFE = FCFF + Net\ Debt\ Variation$$

It would have been correct in our analysis of Free Cash Flow **but erroneous in the sense of dividend estimation**. In effect, if a company can theoretically increase its debt in order to pay a dividend, they will hardly ever do so. It is very risky to follow this strategy, since debt must be financed and usually corresponds to a way of financing a project, an investment, etc. that generates Cash-flows to reimburse the debt. Dividends are just a cash outflow that generates no direct Cash-flow. And paying dividends with debt is a way of takings the wealth of debt investors to give it to equity investors, meaning it almost is a scam.

One example is when a company increases its debt by vast amounts and still is not expected to pay any dividend for the considered period. It happens when a company buys another one. The higher the paid price in cash, the fewer are the chances that it will pay any dividends, and that even if the debt it recently emitted is several times the amount of cash dividend it pays each year.

I would add that if a company has to emit debt in order to pay its dividends, it is probably that it goes through a difficult time and probably that it already is fully leveraged. At best its debt ratio is already poor, at worst covenants forbid to pay any dividend already. It is also the responsibility of shareholders to endure a dividend cut since dividends must be considered as equity and must face the same advantages and drawbacks of equity (shareholders get a higher return on their investments to compensate for higher risks).

For all these reasons, we chose to separate the net debt variation from the Free Cash-flows analysis and used a Free Cash-flows to the Firm model instead of a Free Cash-flows to Equity model.

Example: AnheuserBusch and Inbev merger[62].
In November 2008, AnheuserBusch announced its will to merge with Inbev, creating the largest beer company in the world at the time. The deal, which was valued at around USD 62.0 Bn and paid in cash, was financed partly via a capital increase and partly via a debt emission. Interests-bearing loans and borrowings jumped from around EUR 5 Bn in 2007 to around EUR 35 Bn in 2008. If we had taken the cash flow from financing, it would have skewed the FCF to around the same it was the previous year (ceteris paribus, CAPEX were around EUR 40.0 Bn and cash flow from financing around EUR 40.0 Bn), and thus the dividend should have been of the same amount as the previous year.

That did not happen for two reasons: the first reason is dilution: with the capital increase, the number of stocks had dramatically increased (by 50%), so if the amount of payable dividends had stayed the same, the amount of dividend per share would have decreased. Secondly, covenants attached to the debt forbade the payment of any unreasonable dividend.

The interesting part is the study of the dividend per share (DPS) paid by the then AnheuserBusch in the years preceding the merger: the dividends paid in 2008 were 2.7 times higher than those paid in 2007...before falling to a -55% the following year...with 50% more stocks that before the merger[63]. In the end, you can find below the dividends paid by AB-Inbev during these years:

---

[62] http://www.ab-inbev.com/content/dam/universaltemplate/abinbev/pdf/investors/annual-and-hy-reports/2008/AR2008_UK_WEB.pdf

[63] http://www.ab-inbev.com/content/dam/universaltemplate/abinbev/pdf/investors/annual-and-hy-reports/2009/AB_InBev_AR09.pdf

Year	2005	2006	2007	2008
DPS (in EUR)	0.48	0.72	2.44	0.28

The history repeated itself in 2015-2016 when AnheuserBusch-Inbev decided to buy SabMiller. The impact on the dividend was highly commented, and many analysts drew their analysis around the case study of 2008. That is why the two aspects (fundamental analysis and pattern-based analysis) of dividend computation are both very important.

FCFF model

The Free Cash-flow to the firm model starts with a financial document called the **cash-flows statement**. The first step will consist in rewriting and understanding every relevant item and performing a deep analysis on each of them. In no way the cash flow statement of the financial accounts must be used directly to assess the cash-generating capacity of a company.

Let's start with the easy part: FCFF method says that the FCF formula is the following:

$$FCFF = CFO - CAPEX$$

With: CFO = EBITDA – Δ(Working Capital) - taxes

That can be represented in a short table:

EBITDA
- Δ(Working Capital)
- Taxes
- CAPEX
= FCFF

In your model, you will have to assess the expected value of those parameters for the current year (the dividend is supposed to be paid at the end of the year. For the interim dividend, you can make the reasoning for the half year results) throughout the results announcements.

Each future years' financials will have to be estimated by comparison with current and past years' financials, market data (oil price, exchange rate, yield, etc.) etc. With the time passing, every forecast will realize, via the quarterly disclosures (at the beginning of a new year, nothing much is known, but at the third quarterly result, a good approximation of the full year financials can be performed).

Each line of the table must be assessed separately with the following keys:

Intermediary cash-flows items	Tools to assess it
EBITDA	One must use a time series approach with a fundamental analysis on the sector. Start with quarterly EBITDA as a time series, adjusted by the productions factors such as the commodity prices, the current demand and offer etc.
Delta working capital	Tricky part where the analyst will have to deduce from history and macroeconomic factors which way is heading the WC. One must analyze the tendency of economic and production cycles. It is often that the company will disclose such data at the beginning of the year and will update investors throughout the year. Generally, economic difficulties are synonyms of decrease of EBITDA and a sudden increase in WC which will reduce with the reduction of production and the reduction of stocks.

	With economic difficulties that last, the debt increases which increases the negativity of the EBITDA and increases the CFO. **On the longer run, the equation EBITDA – Δ(WC) can be expected not to vary much**.
Other items	Those items can be very important when they are exceptional. When it happens, they must be duly noted in order not to flaw the analysis. They are composed of: - net interests expenses - earnings from equity accounted entities, less dividends received - share based payment, retirement benefits etc. that are often low compared to the rest - other non-operating expenses (for example: a fine).
Taxes	Those taxes are not the same as the taxes of the income statement. They are considered as taxes on the EBITDA and it often happen that their value is a linear function of the value of the EBITDA (a fixed percentage). A deeper analysis can be performed but it is not very relevant (you can apply a fo.
CAPEX	CAPEX is one of the most important items on the cash flow statement. Also called **investment**, CAPEX (or capital expenditure) represents the cash expenses a company makes, in order to be able to produce. It can be the upgrade of a refinery, an acquisition of a smaller company for external growth etc. The impact of this item on the financials can vary from null (a bank has no CAPEX) to large (heavy industries such as oil and gas companies are CAPEX intensive). Industrial companies will often disclose their target CAPEX, as investors cautiously watch this parameter.
FCFF	It is the cash that is generated by the

	activity of the company, by the goods it produces and sells and is considered to be the "purest" form of cash-flows. There is no other way to generate cash from a production point of view. A negative FCFF is often a bad sign for a company, all the more highlighted by the fact that financial valuation is based on the cash-flow generation capacities. A Discounted Cash-flow model will do the exact same analysis but will do it on a business plan based on five years and an analysis performed to infinity.

Focus on CAPEX: gross CAPEX versus net CAPEX:
The word "CAPEX" is the financial word of what everyone calls **investment**. It is a part of the cash flow statement in the part of cash flow from investing activities. The analysis of the CAPEX must be undertaken from a "net" point of view, meaning that the line "CAPEX" represent the net CAPEX.

But what is the difference between gross CAPEX and net CAPEX? It is the **divestment** part. When "spending capital", companies invest in projects whose ultimate goal is to generate cash-flows with a target of profitability higher than the remuneration of shareholders. When profitability is below shareholders' expected returns, the company will be urged to sell those assets to companies that will be better able to use them and generate higher returns. So the company that invested the CAPEX will sell those activities (that can range from a small factory, stakes in projects, etc. to whole subsidiaries) to other actors of the industry and get cash for the sale. This cash will diminish the cash outflow from investment and will be taken into account in the net CAPEX.

A FCF analysis must take into account the net CAPEX since **divesting is part of the production process of a company**. However, sometimes, divestments can be considered as exceptional when their amount exceeds by far what the company is used to divesting. In that case, it is important to note the exception in the commentaries, since large divestment often lead to cash redemption to shareholders (special dividends) that must not be taken into account in the bottom-up analysis.

Last but not least, companies can separate the CAPEX in their financial statements by their nature: from an industrial process point of view, from a raw material point of view etc. It can be interesting to perform such analysis since companies will often tell the reader of the annexes what are the most important points in analyzing this item.

The analysis on indebtedness

As we saw on the FCF analysis, the cash-generating capacity of a company is only based on its production cycle. However there is also another item that can have large impacts on the cash generation: **indebtedness**. Represented by the so-called "cash-flows from financing activities" in the income statement, the capacity for a company to increase and decrease its debt is very important since it is a cash operation. The financial balance is scrutinized by every actor on the financial markets (and not only the bond traders).

By debt, we meant **financial debt**, meaning short term and long term financial debt. **Current debt** (the so-called "payables") **is not considered as financial debt**.

The balance is easy to understand:

- **When emitting new debt**, a company increases its cash balance by (roughly) the amount of the debt it emits
- **When repaying debts**, a company decreases its cash balance by the amount of the repaid debt
- Interests it pays on its debt can become unsustainable and be a burden for a company, however it is rarely the case for large companies and when interest rates are low.

The analysis of emitting and reimbursing debt must be performed by the analyst and is quite complicated since companies are supposed to be able to emit as much debt as they want[64]. Debt emission cannot be used as a *deus ex machina* by analysts to explain the increase of the cash balance. And it is very rare that a company will take the risk of emitting debt to pay a dividend if they have no other financial resources. In the end, in a period of slow growth, when the company has reached maturity, the balance generated by debt emission and repayment must be equal to zero.

A fast increase of debt emission that is not followed by reimbursement is not necessarily a bad sign, it can be that the company is planning an external acquisition, and is thus piling-up cash. Last but not least, a company can emit new debt in order to repay an existing tranche that has a higher coupon rate.

Focus: net debt versus gross debt

Emission and repayment of debt must be analyzed in the same way CAPEX are. Debt emission is only dangerous when not controlled, and if the amount already emitted is large considering the size of the company.

That is why, when performing the debt analysis, one must also take into consideration the **net debt of the company**. The net debt is **the outstanding debt decreased by the amount of <u>available</u> cash and other financial assets held on the balance sheet**. By doing so, the analyst can evaluate the net change in the amount of debt. The net amount does not change if the emitted debt is held as cash on the balance sheet.

An assessment of the cash items of the balance sheet is necessary. One must only use the line "cash and other cash equivalents" as available cash. **An analysis of non-liquid cash items must be performed** and a warning must be made if the

[64] They could theoretically emit as much debt as they want, in order to pay a dividend.

company does not use enough caution and gives a "cash qualification" to an item that should not be granted such qualification.

Having done the computation of net debt, the analyst will be urged, when analyzing quarterly results, to make a crossed analysis: gross debt increase, gross debt decrease, net debt increase and net debt decrease. The aim is to explain the increase/decrease of indebtedness with the impact of emission/redemption of financial liabilities, and doing the same on the cash increase/decrease. By doing that, you will have a **cross-analysis on indebtedness**.

Focus on debt covenants

Creditors are a type of stakeholders that have seniority versus stockholders of a company. As such, they will be paid the interests and the nominal of debts before every other creditor is paid. **Should the company have troubles paying back its debt** (principal or interest), **some covenants exist in order to forbid the company to pay dividends**. One typical example is when a company merges with another: if it buys the company with cash raised through debt, the bank consortium will ask guarantees such as the suspension of dividend for the delay of repayment.

Oftentimes, **those covenants are in term of financial ratio**: for example, if the ratio debt/EBITDA goes above 3, the dividend is suspended etc. When a company is in trouble due to its financial burden, dividends cut can be automatic even if there are no covenants attached to the debt: **the larger the amount of dividends paid is important, the more interesting for the company a dividend cut will be** (if a dividend represent 15% of the total financial debt, it can be very interesting to cut it).

That principle reminds us the priority of creditors in front of shareholders, and that, basically, **dividends behave more like stocks than like bonds' coupons**.

Last but not least, **companies will automatically disclose the specifics of their financial liabilities** such as the nature of the bonds, their tranches, their nominal, their maturity, their duration, etc. **but not the covenants attached to them** since it often is a private agreement between the company and its creditors. However they can disclose it when asked, so do not mind paying a phone call to the Investors Relations.

Conclusion

The analysis of the cash-flows statement is probably the most sensitive matter on dividend analysis. Every company, all the more if they are troubled, will use "techniques" to hide non-performing balance sheets. Those tricks must be spotted really fast and eliminated from the analysis.

The most common tool is the "**window dressing**" that troubled companies often use. A few weeks before the financial statements are published, they will emit new debt and put the money on their balance sheet (they don't spend it, they just keep it in their books). The unsuspecting financial analyst will then apply the theory he learned and compute the cash balance, the net debt and every ratios derived from the net debt[65]. Nothing will strike much: no increase in net debt (let's say the company emits EUR 1.0 Bn of financial liabilities and puts the EUR 1.0 Bn on its balance sheet, the net debt remain steady), increase in the cash position, and no impact on the ratios explainable from the net debt (since the net debt does not vary). Overall the impact would even be positive for the company!

But we can also give the example of a certain Italian oil and gas company that discloses its financial statements with different currencies to hide the weak balance sheet and management issues...

---

[65] See the ratio at the end of the book.

And when companies write in their reports the words “strong balance-sheet” or “strong capital generation”, **there is a high probability it is a phony statement**.

7

Concrete applications

Introduction

In this part, we will give you several key pieces of information to compute dividends. We took three much studied sectors as examples: the integrated oil and gas sector, the metal and mining sector and the banking sectors.

Oil and gas, mining companies

The **oil and gas sector**, constituted of integrated oil and gas companies, and the **metal and mineral sector**, also called mining sector, or commodity sector, are two very volatile and also very predictable sectors. Very volatile because their values derive from the price of raw materials they extract from the ground (also called: natural resources), but also predictable since **there is a high correlation between the performance of the stock and the evolution of the price of raw materials**. And as I already told the reader, this sector is particularly well fitted for sectorial analysis.

The best example of the mix is the company **BHP Billiton**: it is considered as a metal and mining company since most of its EBITDA comes from metal and mining operations, but it also produces oil (it does not refine it, though) at a large quantity (around 600kboe/d[66] in 2015) which **makes it the fourth largest oil producer in Europe** (at the same level of Repsol **after** the Talisman acquisition in 2015).

Oil and gas specificities

Cash-Flows from Operations: the CFO directly derives from the oil price, **in an almost linear way**: the higher the oil price, the higher the EBITDA and thus the CFO.

This assertion must be detailed further:
The oil and gas industry is actually composed of **three separate industries**: the **upstream** (also called exploration and production), the **downstream** (also called refining) and the **marketing and services**[67] [68].

The technicality is that upstream is an increasing function of the oil price (the higher the oil price, the higher the profit), while downstream is a decreasing function of the oil price (the higher the oil price, the lower the profits). Moreover, upstream has

---

[66] Kboe/d = thousands of barrels of oil equivalent per day.

[67] That is why we call the companies « **Integrated oil and gas** », meaning **they control the whole value chain**.

[68] Some companies aggregate their Marketing and Services division into Downstream.

often a higher share of profit when the oil price is high than the downstream has when the oil price is low. As such, the EBITDA of oil and gas companies is mainly determined by the upstream division.

Analysts have to estimate the EBITDA with an econometric model. An easy way to do it is to build an equation with one parameter (the oil price[69]) and one output (the EBITDA) based on the historical values of the couples oil price/EBITDA. It is very gross analysis but it fits the basic needs for financial estimation.

If the analyst wants to be more precise, he can use a model with **two variables: the oil price** (for upstream earnings), **the refining margin**[70] (for downstream earnings) and **the marketing services income** (that can often be approximated with a constant).

Modeling the oil price impact on a company's financials can be summed-up with a function like:

$$\pi = \alpha X^2 + \beta X + \gamma$$

X: price of oil (you do not take into account the refining margin)
π: profit of the company in a larger sense (can also be the breakeven point)

<u>**The excise tax**</u>: it can be easily computed by hands and is a share of total earnings (often around 10%) and is a **tax on the volume instead of on added value**. It is applied to a determined type of goods and its best illustration is the oil and gas sector.

---

[69] The analysis must be performed on a corresponding period. The oil price to be taken is the average oil price of the considered period. It is a data that every oil and gas companies share, and is the average price of the Brent for European companies.

[70] The margin gained by refiners: the lower the oil price, the higher the margin.

CAPEX: they are the backbone of the industry since they represent the largest amount of cash outflows. It is probably the financial statement that is the most disclosed and commented by companies. CAPEX basically represent investments made by a company. In the Oil and Gas sector, it is the money that is poured into new wells (cost of the technology for discoveries, the cost of well drilling, the cost of extraction, etc.) or used to build and keep up-to-date the refineries.

It can be compared to blood for the human body to work, with the difference that these CAPEX are cash spendings that are made once for all. It is impossible to get them back when they are spent since they are not necessarily activated when expended (although some of them eventually become assets that can be sold). That means that if an exploration program is not successful, the money spent for it is lost forever. And it can amount for several billion dollars, and at a fast pace. **There is a huge bias that increases the amount spent**: when a company already spent billions, it can be urged to spend a little more to pursue the research while stopping the funding would make the project fail and all the money spent would be lost.

That is exactly why a large discovery made by one company is great for the company but can end up being a bottomless pit if it cannot be exploited right away or with difficulties. Shared projects mean that profits but also risks are spread between different players and thus are very appreciable in times of struggles with the project.

CAPEX is a crucial parameter as well as a major expense in the income statement, and integrated oil and gas companies will want to control it. We saw that dividends are paid with free cash-flows that are computed with:

$$FCF = CFO - CAPEX$$

Since CFOs are a function of the oil price and the company has no power on it, it will have a direct influence on CAPEX in order to maximize the FCF. **For example, if the oil price decreases too much, the FCF are at risk to become negative (CFO lower than CAPEX) and thus the company will try to curb its CAPEX in order to make a profit.**

However, CAPEX are not very flexible, all the more that they are subject to currency fluctuation: since the costs are mostly in dollars (USD), any strengthening of the USD in front of the euro or the Great Britain pound (GBP) increases the spending in the local currency. **And even if financial statements are disclosed in USD[71], dividends are paid in the local currency** (the Euro (EUR) and the British Pound for European companies). Meaning that:

- If a company FCFs remain constant in USD, it will lower in EUR if the EUR strengthens compared to the USD;
- A company makes profit in USD and in local currencies, while it costs are in USD. Thus if the USD strengthens[72] compared to local currencies, the profit will suffer negative currency effects.

And currency effects are included on the equity statement rather than in the income statement, and they are considered as cash items. They are located at the bottom of the cash-flow statement, along with the variation on the considered period of time. I recommend the reader to study that part in details since it can become tricky.

Every detail of the industry and their impact on oil and gas companies' earnings is detailed in the Appendix 4 at the end of this book. It comprises of an in-depth analysis on the customs of the industry and some explanations on how valuation works, how reserves are computed, why CAPEX is a more important data than just for financial analysis, and much more.

---

[71] With the exception of Ente Nazionale di Idrocarburi, ENI.

[72] Which happened in 2015.

Metal and mining specificities

Those companies are **often constituted of an upstream division that is responsible for extracting the minerals, and a downstream unit that is in charge of selling the goods on the market**. The latter can be very developed in the form of the large commodity traders (such as: Trafigura, Vitol, Mercuria), and there is one notable example, Glencore (former Glencore Xstrata), which has the particularity of being a producer and a trader, and it even has an agricultural commodities branch. It is the largest (and the only) integrated mining company in the world. The idea behind the merger of the two entities is to mitigate the risk of one arm with the other.

Other companies are not as much diversified as Glencore, they basically produce different ores and minerals, and sell them to trading companies. There has been a huge change in the industry's composition due to the commodity rout of 2015, parts of those companies have been demerged (South32 for BHP Billiton, the agricultural trading firm of Glencore, the De Beers Company from Anglo American, etc.).

Those companies were very successful when prices of raw materials were high, until the recent years. They have then known several downturns and were the **biggest losers of the 2015 commodity rout**. They were also **heavily indebted**, the combination of huge debt and weak earnings made them the perfect example for dividend cuts that occurred in 2015.

Financial institutions

Capital reinvestment[73]

The Financial Institutions sector (meaning: banks and insurance companies) is one of the most difficult sector to evaluate. Every aspects of this sector are meant to make the work of analysts difficult. **The most difficult thing to apprehend is the asymmetry of information between the banks' insiders and people out of it** (clients, investors, regulating bodies, etc.). The perfect example is how the bank evaluates its portfolio: let's take credit portfolios: they are evaluated with prudential rules that are a mix between regulatory constraints and internal models that are discretionary to the banks[74]. It is not uncommon to hear a bank suddenly discovering financial assets that they are unable to evaluate, and in fear that it is worth nothing, they register in the financial statements at the acquisition cost (or historical cost to be precise) while it should be valued at fair-value cost. Or have a deeply illiquid portfolio whose value is the historical cost.

Anyway, for that reason, it is very difficult to assess the risk of equity and especially on the dividend: every pieces of information are not necessarily public and available to everyone, and it is not in the best short-term interest of the bank to disclose every data[75].

The other thing that is difficult to apprehend for a bank is the way it generates money. Basically, it emits long term debt, it

---

[73] We suggest you read "Investment Valuation - Tools and Techniques for Valuing Any Asset", Chapter 21 "Valuing Financial Service Firms" by Aswath Damodaran. The explanation he gives on the way financial services firms work is great.

[74] I recommend the reader to read this excellent article from Matt Levine published by Bloomberg BusinessWeek: "Bank of America Made $168 Million Last Quarter, More or Less" (available freely on Bloomberg's website).

[75] Technically, hiding fundamental pieces of information, such as losses from credit portfolios, is considered as a fraud. However the public is the latest informed of those elements, when it already is too late.

lends on the shorter term, and the difference between the terms is the gross income. To that, one can add gains from the fees the clients pay[76], and the gains on financial markets. If you then subtract the exploitation cost of the bank (the cost of branches, the cost of labor of its workforce, the bonuses, etc.) and any other one-off item (example: a large fine)[77], you get the net income attributable to shareholders that is basically a cash balance[78].

But in order to grow, a bank must increase the number of loans it grants, and each new loan requires a sum of money to be put apart for prudential reasons, the amount being enacted by regulators. The money is not technically cash, but rather what we call capital (constituted by shareholders equity, etc.). **And the only ways to increase that level of capital is whether to "reinvest" a part of the net income into the capital** (= appropriation of the net income, or retained earnings, attribution of the net income to shareholders' equity) **or make a capital increase through financial markets.**

Since the second solution is not a sustainable one, it is mandatory for banks to reinvest part of their result into the capital in order to grow[79].

The part that is not reinvested can be distributed as dividends to the shareholders. This amount is often called "**Maximum Distributable Amount"** [80].

$$MDA = profit - retained\ earnings$$

[76] For example: fees to have an account, to transfer the money to foreign countries, withdrawal fees, fees from a negative balance etc.
[77] That part is amongst the most difficult things to apprehend.
[78] It is not really a cash balance, but apart from depreciation of assets, many items are cash, or have a direct impact on the capital of the bank.
[79] The other possible analysis is that the business of the bank is decreasing, in that situation, there will be an excess of capital that the bank will be able to give back to its shareholders.
[80] See the book by Aswath Damodaran (see note 67).

This distributable amount is thus the excess of capital than can be returned to the shareholders. That is why we call every model derived from this theory: **return of excess capital** models. This can also be used to evaluate a whole bank. Instead of discounting free cash-flow, the analyst will **discount the annual excess of generated capital**.

The various metrics of the bank's capital position

We just explained that financial regulation demanded some capital to be reinvested in the bank in order to sustain its growth. To be more precise, the capital demanded is of high quality, meaning it can only be:

Share premium
Retained earnings
Other comprehensive income
Dividends (-)

The only way to increase its capital (except by capital increase), is **to allocate more earnings to retained earnings**. The capital of highest quality is called the "**Common Equity Tier 1**" (abbreviated in CET1). It is used in a prudential ratio called the "**Common Equity Tier 1 ratio**" (abbreviated in CET1 ratio), whose formula is:

$$CET1\ Ratio = \frac{CET1}{RWA}$$

RWA is the "**Risk-weighted Assets**", which is a regulatory measure of the assets of a bank. The computation of the RWA will not be explained here, let us say that, in order to compute it, a bank multiples its exposures on the balance by a factor that is representative of the risk of each underlying assets.

For example, a AAA German Bund will have a factor of 0, meaning having a Bund on its balance sheet is the same as having nothing if you measure of the risk of the balance sheets. The lower the risks the lower the RWA, the lower the total amount of capital needed, and the less costly it will be for the bank.

Let's sum it up: **if a bank's RWA increases over a year** (for example if it loans more money to customers), **at constant CET1, the CET1 ratio will decrease**. However if the regulator demands a minimum CET1 ratio, **the bank could be required to put more capital aside** (meaning some results) and thus potentially limit the dividends payment (a larger share of results would go to the capital and the remaining parts would be distributed).

Computing the dividend of a bank[81]

Starting with the theory of capital reinvestment, we can build a small model to compute the dividend payable by a bank, knowing that dividends are a share of the capital generated during the year. To be precise, the **maximum payable amount** for the dividend is the amount of generated capital when every reinvestments and restatements have been made (basically capital reinvestment).

[81] We suppose here that the dividend is in cash. When paid in scrip and mainly elected as stock, it is quite different since the problem of dilution and potentially high yield steers the bank decision when paying a dividend.

Let us take an example: (in m)

Y(n-1) data		Y(n) data expected	
RWA	454,500	RWA	477,225
CET1 **after** net inc. attribution	54,540	CET1 **before** net inc. attribution	54,540
CET1 ratio end of year	12%	Target CET1 ratio	12%
Net income	4,300	Expected net income	4,500
		Mandatory capital reinvestment[82]	2,765
		Capital available for dividend payment[83]	1,735
		CET1 ratio before capital reinvestment	11.43%
		CET1 ratio after capital reinvestment	12%

Comment: if the company has 1.2 Bn stocks, we can add:

Maximum dividend payable before capital reinvestment	3.75
Corresponding payout ratio	100%
Maximum dividend payable after capital reinvestment	1.45
Corresponding payout ratio	38.7%

Last but not least, let us imagine that the company said it would pay out at least 40% of its net income attributable to shareholders. In this situation, it would have been impossible

---

[82] = target CET1 ratio x RWA – CET1 bef. Distribution = 12% x 477225 - 54540

[83] = expected net income – mandatory capital reinvestment = 4500 - 2765

since the maximum payable dividend corresponds to a 38.7% payout ratio.

It is obvious that the analysis we just performed is very (too much?) simple. **In reality, banks will have various business strategies and ties with shareholders to take into account,** when deciding the dividend to be paid. They are also very sensitive to any depreciation of goodwill generated from subsidiaries, any depreciation of their loans portfolio, any restructuring costs and other non-interests expenses.

Elements that impact the dividend

The cost of risk

The cost of Risk is calculated by **comparing the total adjustments on impaired assets included in the income statement with the overall outstanding of loans to the customers**. The amount, in percentage, represents the credit that will never be recovered by the bank and is considered as a loss. An increasing cost of risk will significantly reduce the net banking income.

Non-interest expenses

Non-interest expenses are expenses that are **not related to the economic activity of the bank**, they are comprised of employee wages, fixed costs, such as property costs, and other exceptional items that harm the profitability (a fine, the costs of compliancy, etc.). Here the two examples of non-interest expenses that are scrutinized when analyzing banks profitability. The amount of these in the income statement can be huge and they are the number threats analysts must check.

Expense	Explanation
Litigations	Expenses to settle judiciary actions (fines, lawsuits, etc.) and the associated costs: lawyers, compliance staff, etc. They are rarely one-off: if a litigation cost emerges, it will remain in the income statement until the compliance service has caught-up and fines have been paid.
Goodwill impairments/intangibles impairments	Impairments performed when the fundamental value of a subsidiary/any intangible asset is too much far away from its acquisition cost.

Those two elements are very difficult to assess, however they often reproduce in time. When a subsidiary value is partially impaired one year, it can be expected to be impaired the following years.

You will find below some illustration (source: Deutsche Bank Investors Relations page[84])
First, you will find below an extract of the 2011 annual report of Deutsche Bank that accurately describes the importance of estimates in analyzing the financial statements (related to litigations).

> Legal and Regulatory Contingencies and Uncertain Tax Positions
> The Group conducts its business in many different legal, regulatory and tax environments, and, accordingly, legal claims, regulatory proceedings or uncertain income tax positions may arise.
>
> The use of estimates is important in determining provisions for potential losses that may arise from litigation, regulatory proceedings and uncertain income tax positions. The Group estimates and provides for potential losses that may arise out of litigation, regulatory proceedings and uncertain income tax positions to the extent that such losses are probable and can be estimated, in accordance with IAS 37, "Provisions, Contingent Liabilities and Contingent Assets" or IAS 12, "Income Taxes", respectively. Significant judgment is required in making these estimates and the Group's final liabilities may ultimately be materially different.

Extract from Deutsche Bank 2011 annual report

[84] https://www.db.com/ir

Second, a table of Deutsche Bank litigation costs and goodwill impairments, compared to profit and dividend payment.

Fiscal year	2016	2015	2014	2013	2012	2011	2010
Net profit	- 1 356	- 6 772	1 691	681	315	4 300	2 300
Dividend per share	-	-	0,75	0,75	0,75	0,75	0,75
Litigation + goodwill impairment	3 653	10 994	2 082	3 180	4 507	655	151
Split:							
Litigation	*2 397*	*5 218*	*1 971*	*3 036*	*2 607*	*655*	-
Goodwill impairment	*1 256*	*5 776*	*111*	*144*	*1 900*	-	*151*

Net profit versus Litigation costs and goodwill impairments, Deutsche Bank, FY2010-FY2016

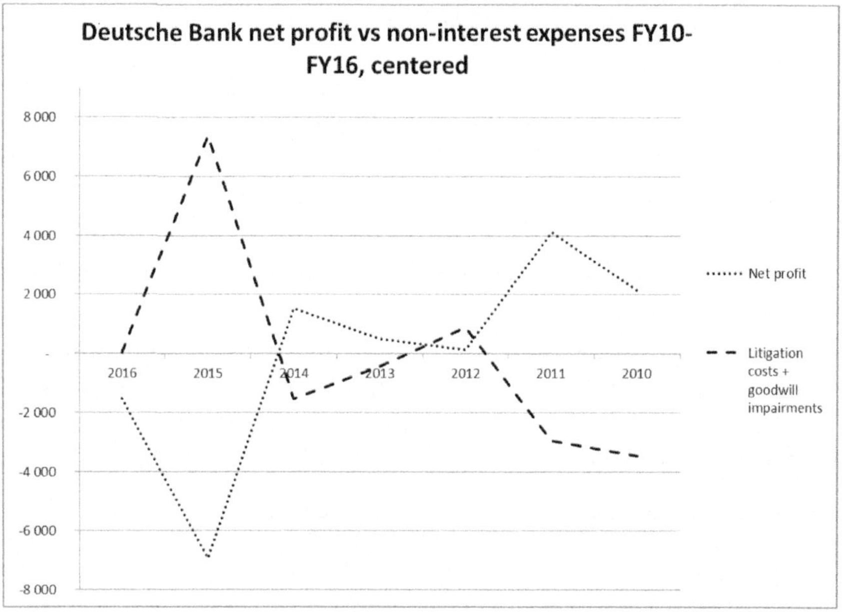

This chart illustrates the tight relation between net profit versus non-interests expenses (litigation costs + goodwill impairments)

Conclusion on financial institutions modeling

Dividend assessment for banks is quite hard because of the structure of the bank. While the profitability of a bank must be studied, the second important metric is the **capital** and how the bank manages it. Considered as a **scarce resource**, a lack of it can prevent the bank from paying a dividend. In excess, it gives the bank much more confidence on it business (the bank can add more leverage to it operation, or more endeavor) and the amount of the payable dividend can be huge considering its other metrics.

On the possibility of paying scrip dividends, **remember that the trade-off between advantages and drawbacks of paying this kind of dividend also concerns banks**, and the matter is often followed by the analysts. The case of Santander is the perfect example where a dividend cut actually meant more capital outflows[85] [86].

To go further: what are the impacts of an interest rate increase on bank's profitability?

1. The mechanism of credit distribution

People who want to buy a house will take out a loan at their local bank, on a long term (usually from 10 to 25 years). **Their loans will carry an interest rate α that is higher than the rate β at which the bank refinances this loan to the central bank (α > β).** This is due to the fact that long-term rates are higher than short-term rate (in a well-functioning economy), and to the fact that the loan rate embeds the cost of money and a premium attached to the profile of the client.

---

[85] We advise the reader to study this case very closely since it reveals the dilemma around scrips.

[86] Santander used to pay a 60ct scrip dividend. It announced in early 2015 that it would be paying a 20ct dividend (two-third cut in value) in cash. While the dividend price was divided by three, paying the dividend in cash resulted in a cash outflow of three times what it used to be when it was a scrip (the scrip had a very high election ratio, meaning most of it was paid in stocks, and thus the cash outflow was limited).

Other elements needs to be taken into account to assess the global balance of credits of a bank: variable-rates loans versus fixed-rate loans, the existence of mortgages (not every country mortgages house credits), early redemptions, profiles of the bank's clients, the economic period the world is going through (**credit growth versus credit crunch**), etc.

2. Two theories on the impact of an increase in rates

- Banks benefit from an increase in interests rates since their margins are higher when interest rates are high
- Or banks suffer from an increase since it is harder to refinance the loans they already emitted at lower interest rates (their margins will reduce or become lower than the cost of risk)

3. Conclusion

- Banks are **more profitable when interests rates are high**, but the process of **interest rate increase can be painful**;
- **Increasing interest rates should have a positive impact on banks that lend at a variable rate**, however this impact should be moderate due to the competition between banks to attract new customers
- **Increasing interest rates should have a negative impact on banks that lent at a fixed rate**, since their costs of refinancing will increase while this increase will not be transmitted to existing clients via an increase in existing loans' interest rates. The margin will only improve when new credits at higher rates are taken out and the number of those credits overcomes existing credit with lower interest rates.

8

Analyzing the quarterly results

Introduction

We have seen, in the three previous parts, several tools to compute dividends and to assess their values. In the everyday job, the analyst will have three ways of computing the dividend:

- The first one is by building from scratch his financial models, which are basically the same as in Equity Research or M&A, except that there will be no discounted free cash-flows but rather a statement of cash-flows for the next two or three following years
- During the quarterly updates of results (the most important one being the Fiscal Year results in February and March), analysts will update their financial models and their estimations with the latest figures of financials. Warning: dividends are announced at the Full Year, so

analysts must produce the estimates for the current year at the latest **before** December expiry

- Or **whenever there is an announcement** (good or bad) that has an impact on the dividend: corporate actions (merger, acquisition), public announcements (fines, profit warning), etc.

The first way is in the analyst's hands, so is the third. In this part, we will give some clues for the second way (results announcements).

Results announcement: what to look for

We have chosen to give you the example of an industrial company and a bank. This analysis can be performed to any sector.

Energy companies[87]

Data	• Oil price, gas price, ERMI (European Refining Margin Indicator) • Upstream production • Downstream production, refinery throughputs, utilization rates • Marketing and services, trading • EUR/USD exchange rate
Results (income statement)	• Net result, Q1-Q4, FY net results • CCS (current cost of supplies) • Adjusted net income, adjusted fully-diluted • Upstream profit • Downstream profit • Marketing & Services profit
Cash-flows statement	• Cash Flow from Operation versus net income, working capital

[87] See http://www.total.com/en/investors/results-and-outlook/main-indicators-historical-information for example of Total's historical data

	• Gross CAPEX, divestment, net CAPEX • FCF balance negative/positive free cash flow versus CFO, CAPEX, CAPEX reduction • The breakeven price of refining • Consumption of debt, debt repayment • Dividends and share buybacks
Indebtedness (balance sheet)	• Net debt • Cash and cash equivalent • Gross debt • Gearing and debt-to-equity ratio • General comments on indebtedness, sustainability of the debt • Covenants
Conclusion and outlook	• Comments on the results • Outlook: CAPEX guidance, oil price ("outlook" parts on annual reports)
Update of the model	• Cash flow from financing • CFO • CAPEX, disposal ⇨ Net CAPEX • CFF

Banks

Data	• Any outstanding data: merger and acquisition, change of CEO, regulatory tightening etc.
Performance	• Net income attributable to shareholders, profit = before tax, any one-off tax • Return on equity • Performance in CIB: retail / securities / Wealth Management, etc.
Non-interest expenses	• Impairment on consolidated subsidiaries • Other impairments • Litigation costs and expenses • Bonuses

Balance sheet	• Total assets, RWA • CET1 ratio, Fully Loaded • Leverage ratio, CET1
Capital management	• Capital raise • Dividend • Share repurchase (no SR in banks though) • Capital shortfall
Update of the model	• Target RWA • Target CET1 ratio • Capital needs for the year to come

Financial ratios

The last step of financial modeling is studying **financial ratios**. This part is similar to credit risk analysis, but less focused on the debt sustainability and more on the covenants part: the aim is to **check that ratios are good enough so that the covenants do not exercise**. Many dividend cuts are due to high leverage ratios, while the business and Cash-flow generation is sound. Our analysis is also a bit different, for we present one ratio that is not usually studied in other books, that is solely relative to dividend sustainability (cash/cash dividend).

Ratio	Explanation
Net debt/EBITDA[88]	It is an illustration of the extent of the repayability of a debt from a cash generating point of view (the EBITDA being the gross cash flow). The higher the ratio, the higher a dividend cut is expected. Beyond 3x is a critical threshold for covenants to exercise and the dividend not to be paid.
Net debt/equity	= gearing. It illustrates the indebtedness of a company, relative to its equity.
CFO[89]**/Interests**	This ratio gives an indication of the

[88] Earnings before interests, taxes, depreciation and amortization.
[89] Cash-flows From Operations.

	capacity for a firm to pay the debts interests. It is a good sign of debt sustainability.
Cash/Cash dividend	**This metric is amongst our favorite**: it gives the coverage ratio of the dividend payment compared to the reserve of cash (it simulates a liquidity crisis were there would be no cash inflow and dividend outflow). It also indicates, *ceteris paribus*, the number of years for the cash balance to be depleted. Below 100%, the situation is desperate (the company will have to borrow money to pay its dividends), and subject to a dividend cut. A ratio of at least 400% is fair.

Financial debt management

Last but not least, **companies will disclose a lot of information on their debt rating and maturity, the bonds they emitted**, etc. They give quite precise description of them, including the redeem date and if they are *callable/putable*, so that the analyst can anticipate a redemption and the necessity to emit new ones. For example, if a debt is paid back during the current year, there is slight risk of dividend cut (however it usually is replaced by a new debt).

Another piece of information that the companies will disclose is the **credit line** they may have with their banks. It is a tool to reassure investors, it corresponds to **short term credit facilities** that can be drawn at any time and are only used in case of emergency. **When used, it is not a very good sign for the financial health of a company**. The bank will have to serve the demanded amount.

9

Conclusion

This book presented via theories and practical examples how to evaluate dividends. It also introduced the reader to a specific new model, the **Dividend Valuation Model**, which theory is for the first time detailed in a book. The reader can build his own dividend valuation models by following the steps detailed in this publication:

- 1- Estimate the amount, based on the global policy of the company
- 2- Assess the capacity of paying a dividend in regard of its income statement
- 3- Assess the capacity in regard of its balance sheets – including debt covenants

The whole information given in this book is yours for the taking; it is up to each reader to make his own models to defy markets.

I hope you enjoyed your reading and do not hesitate to contact me to gabriel.jablon@gmail.com if you have any question on this subject or want to share your knowledge.

Appendix

Appendix 1: STOXX methodology guide

9. STOXX BLUE-CHIP INDICES

9.2. EURO STOXX 50

9.2.1. OVERVIEW

The EURO STOXX 50 is derived from the EURO STOXX index and represents the largest Supersector leaders in the Eurozone in terms of free-float market capitalization.

Universe: The index universe are stocks in the Eurozone region defined by the EURO STOXX index.

Weighting scheme: The index is weighted according to free-float market capitalization.
Base value and dates: 1000 on December 31, 1991.
Index types and currencies: Price, gross return and net return in EUR, USD, CAD, GBP and JPY.
For a complete list please consult the data vendor code sheet on the website[13].

9.2.2. INDEX REVIEW

Component selection

EURO STOXX 50 index (40 – 60 buffer rule)
Target coverage: 50 Supersector leaders from the EURO STOXX index:

1. For each of the 19 EURO STOXX Supersector indices, the stocks are ranked in terms of free-float market capitalization. The largest stocks are added to the selection list until the coverage is close to, but still less than, 60% of the free-float market capitalization of the corresponding EURO STOXX TMI Supersector Index. If the next highest-ranked stock brings the coverage closer to 60% in absolute terms, then it is also added to the selection list. All current EURO STOXX 50 Index stocks are added to the selection list.
2. All the stocks on the selection list are then ranked in terms of free-float market capitalization to produce the final index selection list.
3. The largest 40 stocks on the selection list are selected; the remaining 10 stocks are selected from the largest remaining current stocks ranked between 41 and 60; if the number of stocks selected is still below 50, then the largest remaining stocks are selected until there are 50 stocks.

The minimum liquidity criteria of the parent index, EURO STOXX index applies.

Review frequency: The index is reviewed annually in September. The review cut-off date is the last trading day of August.

[13] http://www.STOXX.com/download/indices/vendor_codes.xls

9. STOXX BLUE-CHIP INDICES

Weighting cap factors: Components are capped at a maximum weight of 10% quarterly. The weighting cap factors are published on Wednesday two trading days prior to quarterly review implementation using Tuesday's closing prices.

Derived indices:

Category	Index
Ex- Financials (excluding ICB 8000)	EURO STOXX 50 ex- Financials
Ex-Banks (excluding ICB 8300)	EURO STOXX ex- Banks
Country sub-indices	EURO STOXX 50 France, Italy and Spain.
Ex-Country indices	EURO STOXX 50 ex Country (e.g. France, Italy, Germany, Spain...)

The ex-Banks and ex-Financial indices use cap factors of the parent index.

9.2.3. ONGOING MAINTENANCE

Replacements: A deleted stock is replaced immediately to maintain the fixed number of stocks., The replacement is based on the latest selection list that is updated monthly. In case of merger and acquisition where a blue-chip stock is involved, the original stock is replaced by the new stock. If a stock is deleted from the EURO STOXX in between the regular review dates but is still a component of the STOXX Regional TMI, then this stock will remain in the EURO STOXX 50 Index until the next regular review.

Fast exit

The components are monitored for any changes based on the monthly selection list ranking, i.e. on an ongoing monthly basis.
A component is deleted if:

» it ranks 75 or below on the monthly selection list; and
» it ranked 75 or below or below on the selection list of the previous month

The announcement will be on the first trading day of the month after close of markets.
The addition will be announced based on the monthly selection list, i.e. the highest-ranked non-component will be selected. Changes will be implemented on the close of the fifth trading day and are effective the next trading day.

Fast entry

All stocks on the latest selection lists and initial public offering (IPO) stocks are reviewed for a fast-track addition on a quarterly basis. A stock is added, if

» it qualifies for the latest blue-chip selection list generated end of February, May, August or November; and
» it ranks within the lower buffer (ranks 1 - 25) on this selection list

If it is added, the stock replaces the smallest stock in the Blue-Chip Index. The announcement will be on the first trading day of the month after close of markets. The implementation is together with the STOXX Total Market indices.

9. STOXX BLUE-CHIP INDICES

Spin-offs

Each spin-off stock qualifies for addition if it lies within the lower buffer (ranks 1 – 40) on the latest selection list for the index. The spin-off replaces the lowest ranked stock in that index as determined by the selection list.

Qualifying spin-off stocks are added in sequence:
The largest qualifying spin-off stock replaces the original stock in the index.
The next qualifying spin-off stock replaces the lowest ranked stock in the index.
Likewise for the other qualifying spin-off stocks.

Appendix 2: scrip dividend announcement comments

We took as example the dividend announcement of Santander dated from the 14/10/2016. You can access it on: https://www.cnmv.es/Portal/HR/BusquedaHR.aspx (CNMV website) and search for "BANCO SANTANDER, S.A." with the type of news "**Aumentos y reducciones del capital social**".

1. Presentation of the different choices shareholders have:

i) Get new shares of Santander (elect the dividend in share)
ii) Get the dividend in cash (« pago de efectivo »)
iii) Sell this right to a dividend on the market. This right has a market price that can fluctuate and is not guaranteed by Santander.

Buying and selling dividend rights on the market is also a profit source from delta one desks but is very marginal.

Note that there are two fiscal treatments for this scrip dividend that illustrates **why electing the dividend in cash is so popular for Spanish stocks**: the option 1 and 3 are tax-free, while option 2 (dividend in cash) is subject to a 19% tax.

2. Details of the offer

In this part, Santander will disclose every element it used to compute the final amount of the dividend. This can be surprising at first, but the final amount of the dividend can be different from the announced amount (a few cents generally).

a. computation of the reference price

The reference price used for the computation of the final amount of the dividend is called PreCot. It corresponds to the average share price during the 10 days before the publication of the announcement).

Example: in this example, the PreCot is EUR 3.973.

b. the number of rights necessary to receive one share

For any share of Santander current shareholders own, there is a right attached to it. The formula is:

$$num. of\ rights = \frac{NTAcc}{\frac{Importe\ opcion\ alternativa}{PreCot}}$$

With:
NTAcc = number of share before dividend payment
Importe Opcion Alternative = total amount of dividends to be paid

The total amount of dividends to be paid is discretionary and is decided by the company. However you can find an approximation of this amount by computing the announced dividend by the number of existing shares.

For every "*num. of rights*" (here 87) existing shares a shareholder owns, he will receive one new share. This amount is also very useful to compute dilution of each dividend to be paid in scrip:

$$dilution = \frac{1}{num. of\ rights} * election\ ratio$$

Example: in our example, NTAcc = 14.434.492.579 existing shares and the amount of total dividends to be paid is EUR 665m. The number of rights required to receive one share as a dividend is 87.

You can see that total dividends to be paid / number of existing shares ≈ dividend amount (0,045).

Computation of the dilution:
The final election ratio is 89.11%. thus the dilution equal to 1.024% (for one dividend. There are four installments a year for Santander...).

c. the amount of new share to be emitted

$$number\ of\ share\ to\ be\ emitted = \frac{NTAcc}{num.of\ rights}$$

Example: in our example, the number of shares to be emitted = 165.913.707.

d. the final price of the dividend

$$final\ price = \frac{PreCot}{num\ of\ rights + 1}$$

Example: in our example, the final price is 3.973 / (87+1) = 0,045 (rounded amount).

Appendix 3: banking dividends estimation (exemple)

1) Model

	Year	2010	2011	2012	2013	2014	2015	2016	2017	2018	2019
1	Share price	48,13	30,35	42,59	56,65	49,26	52,23	43,23	43,23	43,23	43,23
3	Net Income attributable to shareholders	7 843	6 050	6 564	4 832	157	6 694	5 437	5 519	5 601	5 685
3	RWA	601	614	552	560	614	629,6	629,6	634,5	639,4	644,4
4	Number of shares	1207,7	1197,4	1214,5	1241,3	1241,9	1243	1296	1289	1309	1324
	Effective CET1	9,20%	9,60%	11,70%	11,70%	10,50%	10,90%				
	Target CET1							11,18%	11,45%	11,73%	12,00%
	Capital needs per year (average)							1731	1745	1758	1772
	Declared amount	2,10	1,20	1,50	1,50	1,50	2,31				
2	Effective yield	4%	4%	4%	3%	3%	4%	4,2%	3,7%	3,6%	3,6%
3	Declared payout ratio						43%	45%	45%	45%	45%
4	MDA under regulatory demands	631	3 594	-5 028	4 832	7 525	4 176	3 706	3 774	3 843	3 913

2) Dividend estimation

	Estimated amount	2016	2017	2018	2019
1	Trend on historical amount	2,27	2,55	3,39	5,55
	Weights	*30%*	*30%*	*30%*	*30%*
2	Trend on historical yield	1,81	1,61	1,58	1,56
	Weights	*10%*	*10%*	*10%*	*10%*
3	Declared payout ratio	1,89	1,93	1,93	1,93
	Weights	*10%*	*10%*	*10%*	*10%*
4	MDA under regulatory demand	2,86	2,93	2,94	2,96
	Weights	*50%*	*50%*	*50%*	*50%*

	2016	2017	2018	2019
Average	**2,20**	**2,30**	**2,50**	**3,00**
Weighted average	**2,50**	**2,60**	**2,80**	**3,50**

Appendix 4: integrated oil and gas companies are exposed at different extents to oil price fluctuations

The main drivers of oil and gas companies' Free Cash-Flows are:

- **Economics**
  - Demand
  - Supply
  - Currency effects
- **Financials**
  - The price of the barrel of oil
  - The volume of oil production
  - The refining margin
  - The CAPEX
  - The change in Working Capital
  - And other cash items
- **Geography**
  - The diversity of income
  - The geographic exposure
  - Political issues

The volume of production is disclosed in **kboe/d** or thousand-barrel-equivalent a day. The division that is the most impacted by this metric is the **Upstream** (Exploration and production).
The refining margin, which is function of the price of the barrel and the use of refining capacities (useless capacities will push the margins down). The division that is the most impacted by this metric is the **Downstream** (or Refining).

Impact, on proved reserves, of an increase in the price of oil: An **increase in oil price** leads to an increase in profitability of the existing wells and of future projects. This increase in prices mechanically leads to an increase of the expected CAPEX (via an increase of profits). Since CAPEX allow new projects to be launched and more wells to be discovered, it also increases the data on proved reserves. **Proved reserves are thus a positive function of oil price**.

During the commodity rout of 2015, the number of shale gas wells in the US fell dramatically, because **the fall of the oil price made those wells not profitable**. Each of these wells has a "**breakeven price**" which is the price of oil above which drilling and exploiting a well becomes profitable.

As an opposite, a **decrease in oil price lowers the revenues of upstream divisions** and long term projects see their profitability decrease or even incur large losses for the companies. Should the period of low oil price last, it could lead to a reduction of new projects' development and impairment of current projects.

Impact, on refinery margins, of a decrease in the price of oil:

- **On the short term**: the refinery margin decreases due to over-capacity of refineries (a decrease in the price of oil is whether due to an oversupply or a weak demand, creating stocks of oil that still need to be refined) that creates more competition between producers
- **On the longer term**: the margin increases with capacity adjustment (old refineries are closing, only the most profitable and the most efficient ones stay open)

To sum-up, the low price of oil is not necessarily bad news for integrated oil and gas companies. On the contrary, it must be seen as a strong signal that they must invest in infrastructures that can modulate the production levels, and, more globally, better work to control their costs.

In a low oil price environment, the worst thing companies could face would be being **producers without any refineries** (since the loss of income from Upstream is partly offset by better refining conditions). The other bad situation would be a refining company that faces recurrent short term drops in the oil price, and is **not able to adjust its production infrastructures** fast enough.

Appendix 5: oil and gas dividends (exemple)

1/ give a global assessment of the financial situation of the company

FCF

figures in USD	2013	2014	2015	2016e
EBITDA	35 287	31 212	8 720	12 067
var. BFR	- 6 843	6 925	843	
Other	- 1 037	- 596	11 826	
= CFO	27 407	37 541	21 389	14 432
IS	- 6 307	- 4 787	- 2 256	- 2 366
Net CAPEX	- 19 752	- 19 574	- 17 300	- 10 861
= Adj. FCF	1 348	13 180	1 833	1 205
Net cash used by investing activities	- 19 752	- 19 574	- 17 300	- 10 861
Other	11 897	-	-	-
Cash flow from financing	- 10 400	- 5 266	- 4 535	- 6 734
Cash and cash equivalent				
At the begining of year	19 635	22 520	29 763	26 389
CF variation	2 845	7 914	- 2 702	- 5 528
Exchange rate gain/loss	40	- 671	- 672	- 672
At the end of year	22 520	29 763	26 389	20 189
Dividends paid to Cie SH (included in the computation above)	- 5 441	- 5 850	- 6 659	- 7 610

CAPEX

	2013	2014	2015	2016e
Purchase of PPE	- 24 520	- 22 546	- 18 648	- 13 891
Purchase of intangible assets	- 518	- 310	- 242	- 357
Investments in joint venture	- 111	- 336	- 1 312	- 586
Proceeds from sales of PPE	1 335	1 820	1 066	1 407
Proceeds from sales of intangibles	3 884	1 671	1 726	2 427
Divestments in joint venture	178	127	110	138

Net Debt

	Liabilities	FY 13	FY 14	FY 15	FY 16e
Current	Interest bearing liabilities	- 7 381	- 6 877	- 6 944	- 7 067
	other financial liabilities				
Non-current	Interest bearing liabilities	- 40 811	- 45 977	- 46 224	- 48 535
	other financial liabilities				

	Assets				
Current	Cash and cash equivalent	22 520	29 763	26 389	20 189
	Other financial assets				
Non-current	cash and cash equivalent				
	Other financial assets				

Net Debt	- 25 672	- 23 091	- 26 779	- 35 414

Equity	129 302	111 441	99 119	114 156
non controlling interest				

Financing activities

	2014	2015	2016e
Net repurchase of shares	- 4 589	-	-
Proceeds from long term financing	12 394	8 173	9 590
Repayment of long term financing	- 6 282	- 6 426	- 7 428
Net increase (decrease) in short term debt	- 693	473	- 486
Net increase (decrease) in non-controlling interests	9	- 5	- 10
Dividends paid	- 6 105	- 6 750	- 4 541

Ratio

	2013	2014	2015	2016e
Net Debt	25 672	23 091	26 779	35 414
EBITDAe	35 287	31 212	8 720	12 067
CFOe	27 407	37 541	21 389	14 432
Equity	129 302	111 441	99 119	114 156

Debt/EBITDA	73%	74%	307%	293%
Debt/KP	20%	21%	27%	31%
CFO/Debt	107%	163%	80%	41%
Dividend / Cash available at end of year	24%	20%	25%	38%
Dividend / FCF	403,6%	44%	363%	631%
gearing	17%	17%	21%	24%

2/ forecast for the next year/ the next following years

FCF estimation, y-o-y

Figures in USD	Q1 14	Q2 14	Q3 14	Q4 14	FY 14	Q1 15	Q2 15	Q3 15	Q4 15	FY 15	Q1 16	Q2 16	Q3 16	Q4 16	FY 16
EUR/USD	1,37	1,38	1,33	1,26	1,33	1,14	1,11	1,13	1,12	1,12					
Var.	*1%*	*1%*	*-4%*	*-5%*	*-2%*	*-10%*	*-3%*	*2%*	*0%*	*-16%*					
Brent	108,20	109,70	101,85	76,60	99,09	46,79	56,69	44,01	37,05	45,63	26,97	44,99	41,23	49,00	40,55
Net Inc.	3 528	3 369	1 290	- 4 407	3 780	2 602	- 5 823	47	1 709	- 1 465	- 583	- 1 419	1 620	- 25	- 407
Total CFO	8 231	7 877	9 399	7 247	32 754	1 858	6 286	5 183	5 806	19 133	1 872	3 883	2 508	3 804	12 067
Var.						*-77%*	*-20%*	*-45%*	*-20%*	*-42%*	*1%*				
CAPEX	- 5 891	- 5 499	- 5 256	- 5 900	- 22 546	- 4 636	- 4 529	- 4 357	- 5 126	- 18 648	- 4 381	- 4 283	- 3 379	- 4 515	- 16 558
Disposals	1 021	851	594	1 152	3 618	1 743	577	349	233	2 902	1 195	450	578	1 050	3 273
Other	- 131	- 50	- 154	- 311	- 646	- 156	- 272	- 141	- 985	- 1 554	- 97	- 204	- 186	- 118	- 605
Net CAPEX	- 5 001	- 4 698	- 4 816	- 5 059	- 19 574	- 3 049	- 4 224	- 4 149	- 5 878	- 17 300	- 3 283	- 4 037	- 2 987	- 3 584	- 13 891
Var.						*-39%*	*-10%*	*-14%*	*16%*	*-12%*					
FCF	3 230	3 179	4 583	2 188	13 180	- 1 191	2 062	1 034	- 72	1 833	- 1 411	- 154	- 479	220	- 1 824
Dividend	- 1 427	- 1 572	- 1 122	- 1 729	- 5 850	- 1 709	- 1 691	- 1 718	- 1 541	- 6 659	- 1 099	- 1 169	- 1 161	- 1 112	- 4 541
Dividend paid per share						0,10	0,10	0,10	0,10	0,40	0,10	0,10	0,10	0,10	0,40
FCF Balance					7 330					- 4 826					- 6 365

Dividends timetable and estimation, simplified

Year	2010	2011	2012	2013	2014	2015	2016e	2017e	2018e	2019e
Oil price	73,4	101,3	102,1	99,2	88,0	45,6	40,6	55,0	65,0	70,0
Net attributable income	- 3 719	25 700	11 017	23 451	3 780	- 6 482	- 407	- 1 552	2 335	4 278
Free Cash flow	9 656	- 4 479	7 404	13 245	13 180	1 833	- 1 824	3 135	4 168	4 685
Total amount	2 627	5 291	6 276	6 911	7 168	7 301	7 668	7 919	8 238	8 889
Cash amount	2 627	4 072	5 294	5 441	5 850	6 659	4 715	7 555	7 538	8 040
Stock amount	-	1 219	982	1 470	1 318	642	2 954	365	700	849
Number of shares	18 796	18 977	19 120	18 611	18 200	18 412	19 026	18 880	18 824	18 798
Issued for the share payment	-	165,6	138,4	202,1	165,6	102,8	129,1	129,1	129,1	129,1
Dividend per share	0,14	0,28	0,33	0,37	0,39	0,40	0,40	0,42	0,44	0,47
Per quarter						0,10	0,10	0,105	0,11	0,12

Appendix 6: some examples of dividends

Condensed dividend timetable

Fiscal Year		2007	2008	2009	2010	2011	2012	2013	2014	2015
BNP Paribas	*DPS (in EUR)*	3,26	0,97	1,50	2,10	1,20	1,50	1,50	1,50	2,31
	P/O ratio	39,5%	TBC	32,3%	33,4%	25,1%	29,7%	40,8%	-	45,0%
	Growth in %		*-70,2%*	*54,6%*	*40,0%*	*-42,9%*	*25,0%*	*0,0%*	*0,0%*	*54,0%*
British American Tobacco	*DPS (in GBp)*	66,2	83,7	99,5	114,2	126,5	134,9	142,4	148,1	154
	P/O ratio	62,9%	67,9%	72,6%	78,7%	80,5%	68,9%	69,3%	88,6%	66,7%
	Growth in %		*26,4%*	*18,9%*	*14,8%*	*10,8%*	*6,6%*	*5,6%*	*4,0%*	*4,0%*
Total S.A.	*DPS (in EUR)*	2,07	2,28	2,28	2,28	2,28	2,34	2,38	2,44	2,44
	P/O ratio	39%	37%	66%	50%	45%	43%	50%	58%	60%
	Growth in %		*10,1%*	*0,0%*	*0,0%*	*0,0%*	*2,6%*	*1,7%*	*2,5%*	*0,0%*
AnheuserBusch InBev	*DPS (in EUR)*	2,44	0,28	0,38	0,8	1,2	1,7	2,05	3	3,6
	P/O ratio	79,30%	26,30%	21,30%	33,80%	38,50%	49,80%	57,60%	64,80%	76%
	Growth in %		*-88,5%*	*35,7%*	*110,5%*	*50,0%*	*41,7%*	*20,6%*	*46,3%*	*20,0%*

Index

About the author

GABRIEL JABLON is a consultant in banking regulation, and is specialized in market risks. He graduated from Paris-Dauphine University in 2015 and holds a master degree in Banking and Finance.

The end

Printed in Great Britain
by Amazon

29382707R00079